FARRAGUT

MILITARY PROFILES
SERIES EDITOR
Dennis E. Showalter, Ph.D.
Colorado College

*Instructive summaries for general and expert
readers alike, volumes in the Military Profiles
series are essential treatments of significant and
popular military figures drawn from world history,
ancient times through the present.*

FARRAGUT

America's First Admiral

Robert J. Schneller, Jr.

BRASSEY'S, INC.
Washington, D.C.

Library of Congress Cataloging-in-Publication Data
Schneller, Robert John, 1957–
Farragut : America's first admiral / Robert J. Schneller, Jr.
p. cm. — (Brassey's military profiles)
Includes bibliographical references (p.) and index.
ISBN 1-57488-398-4 (alk. paper)
1. Farragut, David Glasgow, 1801–1870. 2. Admirals —
United States — Biography. 3. United States. Navy —
Biography. 4. United States — History — Civil War,
1861–1865 — Naval operations. 5. United States —
History, Naval — To 1900. I. Title. II. Series.
E467.1.F23 S34 2002
973.7′5′092 — dc21   2002025401

Brassey's, Inc.
22841 Quicksilver Drive
Dulles, Virginia 20166

FIRST EDITION

10 9 8 7 6 5 4 3 2 1

for Mom

Contents

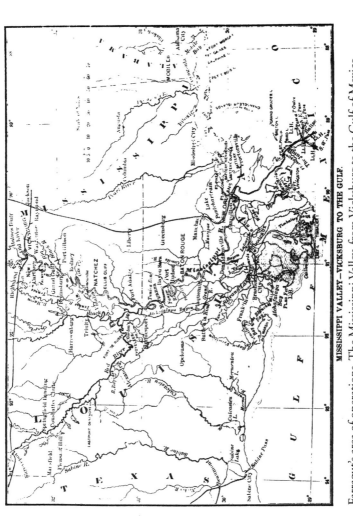

MISSISSIPPI VALLEY—VICKSBURG TO THE GULF.

Farragut's area of operations. The Mississippi Valley, from Vicksburg to the Gulf of Mexico, including Mobile Bay. *Naval Historical Center NH2303*

Maps

Preface

Lashed in the rigging of the *Hartford*'s mainmast high above the deck, Rear Admiral David Glasgow Farragut had a bird's-eye view of his fleet as it fought past the booming guns of Fort Morgan into Mobile Bay. Everything was going according to plan until the monitor *Tecumseh* suddenly rolled to starboard, her bow knifing into the water and stern rearing up with the propeller still spinning, then plunged out of sight like an arrow shot from a bow. Farragut knew instantly that the *Tecumseh* had struck a torpedo, as mines were called in those days. As the gunfire from the Confederate fort intensified, the *Brooklyn,* the lead ship in the main column just ahead of the *Hartford,* started backing down, her skipper reporting a line of torpedoes across the channel.

Farragut realized that the decisive moment had arrived. The column was bunching up under the enemy guns. To try to maneuver around the torpedoes would lengthen the ships' exposure to the cannonade. To go forward would hazard the fleet against the torpedoes. To retreat was out of the question. Farragut reflected on everything he knew about the Confederate defenses, offered a silent prayer, then acted. "Damn the torpedoes!" he shouted. "Full speed ahead!" Farragut led his ships onward that August morning to one of the most celebrated victories in American naval history.

Good naval officers know that the prerequisites for victory include thorough logistical arrangements, intimate familiarity with ships and weapons, and a firm grasp of tactics. But what separates the good officer from the great one is the courage to make difficult decisions in the heat of combat despite personal fear or the awful realization that some of the men will have to pay in blood. "The great man in our country must not only plan, but execute," Farragut once said. "Success is the only thing listened to in this war, and I know that I must sink or swim by that rule."[1]

Farragut's careful preparations, keen situational awareness, and, above all, courage to act boldly at the decisive moment produced the Union's greatest naval victories and resulted in his appointment as America's first admiral. These qualities also made Farragut the greatest naval officer of the Civil War, Union or Confederate, and the greatest American naval officer of the nineteenth century.

This is a military biography of Farragut, not a full biography. It doesn't enumerate his faults, of which he had his share. Nor does it dwell on his family life and personal relationships or probe deeply into his personality. The focus remains on the qualities of leadership that made him great as well as on the moments in his life when his greatness came to the fore.

Many people helped me with this book. I thank Rick Russell, the editor at Brassey's who launched the Military Profiles series. My agent Fritz Heinzen has my gratitude for guiding me through the business side of writing. I'm indebted to Bob Browning and Mark Hayes for suffering through a draft of the entire book and offering valuable suggestions for its improvement. Helping me with books has become a habit with these guys.

My colleagues at the Naval Historical Center deserve profuse thanks. Ed Finney, Jack Green, and Chuck Haberlein of the Photographic Section along with the staff of the Naval Historical Foundation have my gratitude for their assistance with the illustrations. I am grateful to Barbara Auman, David Brown, Davis Elliott, Glenn Helm, Jean Hort, Young Park, and Tonya Simpson of the Navy Department Library for granting my constant requests for books and answering countless reference questions. The service that these people provide is typically excellent. "Above and beyond" seems to be the only call of duty they know.

I am particularly indebted to Jim Cheevers, curator of the Naval Academy Museum, for guiding me through the Museum's collection of Farragut papers and photographs and suggesting other places to look. The staffs of the Library of Congress and National Archives also have my gratitude for their assistance and for preserving America's heritage.

Although these people helped make this book better, responsibility for its flaws remains with me.

Last but not least, I want to thank my wife Rebecca and sons Zachary and Noah for their patience and support during the time I spent with Farragut and not with them.

Chronology

1838, November 27	Witnessed French bombardment of fortress at San Juan de Ulloa
1840, December 27	Death of Susan Farragut
1841, February	Executive officer of *Delaware* (Brazil Station)
1841, September 27	Commissioned commander
1842, June	Command of *Decatur* (Brazil Station)
1843, December 26	Married Virginia Dorcas Loyall
1844, April	Receiving ship, Norfolk
1844, October 12	Birth of son Loyall
1847, March	Command of *Saratoga* (Gulf of Mexico)
1848, February	Second-in-command, Norfolk Navy Yard
1850, October	Ordnance duty (Washington, Norfolk)
1854, August	Ordered to establish Mare Island Navy Yard
1855, September 14	Commissioned captain
1858, December	Command of *Brooklyn* (Caribbean)
1861, April	Moved from Norfolk to Hastings-on-Hudson
1862, January 9	Command of West Gulf Blockading Squadron
1862, April 24	Passed Forts Jackson and St. Philip
1862, April 25	Captured New Orleans
1862, June 28	Passed batteries at Vicksburg
1862, July 15	CSS *Arkansas* passed two Union fleets
1862, July 16	Commissioned rear admiral
1863, March 14	Passed batteries at Port Hudson
1863, July 4	Surrender of Vicksburg
1863, July 9	Surrender of Port Hudson
1863, August 1	Sailed for New York
1864, January 5	Sailed for the Gulf
1864, August 5	Battle of Mobile Bay
1864, November 30	Sailed for New York
1864, December 23	Commissioned vice admiral
1865, April	Visited Richmond and Norfolk
1866, July 25	Commissioned admiral
1867, July 15	Command of European Squadron
1869, Summer	Visited Mare Island Navy Yard
1870, August 14	Died at Portsmouth, New Hampshire

FARRAGUT

Chapter 1

Child of the Frontier

D AVID GLASGOW FARRAGUT was rooted in the American frontier, a son of pioneers and a child of the Old West. He was born on July 5, 1801, in a log cabin on a 640-acre tract of land on the north bank of the Holston River about fifteen miles southwest of Knoxville in the state of Tennessee, which had joined the Union just five years earlier. Although a bit larger and more pretentious than the typical frontier cabin, the Farraguts' house had windowpanes of paper soaked in hog's fat, wooden shutters, a heavy wooden door, and loopholes through the walls for defense against Indian attacks.

David's father, George Anthony Magin Farragut, had settled in Tennessee after fighting the British throughout the Revolutionary War. George first glimpsed daylight on 29 September 1755 on the island of Minorca. His childhood passed pleasantly enough amid red-tile roofs under the warm Mediterranean sun. George grew restless as he grew older and, choosing the natural occupation of an islander, went to sea at the age of ten. He plied the Mediterranean for seven years, including service with the Russian fleet during its great victory over the Turks in the Black Sea in

May 1770. He then shaped a course for the Caribbean and there spent two years trading between Havana and Vera Cruz. Upon hearing that the thirteen American colonies had declared their independence, he decided to risk life and fortune in the struggle against Great Britain. He harbored an ancestral hatred for that country, as the British had ruled Minorca until the year after his birth.

After arriving in Charleston in 1776, George sailed in privateers and rode with guerrilla leader Francis Marion, the famous "Swamp Fox." He fought with Marion at Cowpens and led a volunteer company of cavalry on raids in the rear of Lord Cornwallis's army during its invasion of North Carolina. By the end of the war, he had risen to the rank of major of horse.

After the war, George Farragut returned to the sea. Then, in 1790, his old friend William Blount, governor of the South Western Territory (which later became Tennessee), invited him to Knoxville and appointed him major of militia. Farragut fought Cherokees and Creeks and acquired hundreds of acres of land for his service during the Revolution and as an Indian fighter. Now a 40-year-old man of property, he decided it was time to get married. The woman he chose was 30-year-old Elizabeth Shine.

Elizabeth Shine was born of Irish ancestry on June 7, 1765, near Kinston, North Carolina, on the Neuse River, the fifth of eight children. Afterwards her family moved to what became known as Shine's Ferry on the French Broad River in the South Western Territory, not far from Old Newport.

The mists of time shroud their first meeting. It might have been as early as the Revolution or later, while George was performing his militia duties. Whenever they first met, they married in 1795, moved to Knoxville, and lived in a house George built so strongly that it remained standing until 1903. Here their first child, a son, was born on August 23, 1797. They named him William.

George had purchased the 640 acres near Stony Point the year before William was born. The Farraguts sold their property in Knoxville and moved into the newly built log cabin in 1800. A year later Elizabeth bore George's second son, David Glasgow.[1] Friends called him Glasgow. A sister, Nancy, followed in 1804 and another brother, George, in 1805.

Although Indian massacres were mostly a thing of the past in East Tennessee, Elizabeth Farragut, like other folks living in out-lying settlements, still worried about outlaws and renegades. One day when Glasgow was five, Elizabeth spotted a group of Indians in the distance. She quickly gathered up the children, placed them in the loft of the log kitchen, a separate building standing near the house, and admonished William and Glasgow to keep the little ones quiet. As the Indians approached, Elizabeth locked herself in the house and parleyed with them from inside, hoping to divert their attention from the children's hiding place. After much talking, the Indians said they would leave her alone if she gave them some whiskey. Elizabeth agreed and unchained and unbarred the door. She barely had the door open a crack when one of the Indians stabbed at her with a knife. Elizabeth blocked the blow, slammed the door shut, resecured it, and stood by with an ax until the Indians went away. When the coast was clear she went out to the kitchen to comfort the frightened children.

George returned home within the hour, and when Elizabeth told him what had happened, he flew into a rage. It was all she could do to keep him from rushing headlong after the Indians. He couldn't handle them by himself, she pleaded, there were too many. George calmed down, but his anger didn't fade. He donned his dragoon uniform, mounted his horse, and rode away to get help. He reappeared two hours later with some eight or ten fellow militiamen, then rode off in pursuit of the Indians. Few of the Indians survived George's wrath.

Although George Farragut liked frontier living, he longed to return to the sea. Through the influence of a former Tennessee politician who had recently become governor general of Louisi-ana, George received an appointment in the U.S. Navy as a sail-ing master on March 2, 1807, and orders to New Orleans.

George figured on moving his family there by flatboat. Build-ing the boat took longer than he had anticipated, so he arranged for a young Kentuckian to accompany his family on the long voyage. He then hastened to the "Crescent City" to command of one of the new gunboats constructed in accordance with Thomas Jefferson's antinavalist policy.

The flatboat provided a slow but relatively comfortable means of transportation. It had a flat bottom, a bow slanting forward at 45 degrees, three or four feet of planking around the edge to serve as a bulwark, and a roofed-over portion aft. It was, in essence, a floating homestead, complete with livestock pens, fodder for the animals, provisions for the people, and a house in which they could use their furniture and utensils while traveling.

Elizabeth and the children began their American odyssey on a stunningly beautiful day late in the summer of 1807. Although they had nearly 1,700 miles to go, it was downstream all the way. For the children it was an adventure as grand as any young Samuel Langhorn Clemens would have a quarter century later. The Farraguts floated down the Holston to the Tennessee, down the Tennessee to the Ohio, down the Ohio to the Mississippi, then down the "Father of the Waters" to New Orleans. Along the way Glasgow and his brothers and sister saw great herds of buffalo and flocks of wild turkeys and fished to their heart's content. As for people, at first they spotted only the occasional Indian canoe, but as they drew near their destination, the traffic increased dramatically, ranging from fur-laden canoes to keelboats carrying barrels of grain, whiskey, bacon, ore, and other goods. There were cargoes of cotton too, but cotton would not become king until after the War of 1812. David Glasgow Farragut's first voyage ended some two months after it began, when the flatboat reached New Orleans, where, fifty-five years later, he would emblazon his name in naval annals.

The Farraguts' new home could hardly have differed more from the one they had left behind. From a quiet, sparsely populated region in the near wilderness where most of the people farmed, worshipped in Presbyterian churches, and spoke English, the family had come to a bustling, diverse, and cosmopolitan city of 15,000 inhabitants largely of French, Spanish, or African descent, most of whom worshipped in Catholic churches, and whose occupations ranged from wholesale merchants who lived in luxury to genuine pirates, including the notorious Jean Lafitte. And instead of log cabins dotting a rustic rural landscape, thousands of buildings, many with steep, red-tiled roofs and intricate metalwork at gateways and balconies, crowded upon narrow, poorly drained streets. The city reminded George of Minorca, but to Elizabeth, it might just as well have been a foreign country. Not long after she arrived in New Orleans, Elizabeth bore her husband a fifth child, another daughter, named Elizabeth after her mother.

It was in this strange place that Glasgow's childhood foundered on the rocks of tragedy. Shortly after assuming his duties as sailing master, George befriended fellow naval officer David Porter, who had arrived in New Orleans not long after George. On a hot day during the spring of 1808, Porter, already suffering from consumption, suffered a sunstroke while fishing. George Farragut happened upon his ailing friend while fishing nearby and took him home, where Elizabeth nursed him through what proved to be his final illness. While caring for the dying Porter, Elizabeth too fell ill, stricken with yellow fever. George placed the children with other families to prevent them from catching the dreaded disease. Elizabeth Farragut and David Porter both died on the same day, June 22, 1808.

Elizabeth's death shattered the family. With their mother gone, the younger children remained scattered in different homes, so that George could perform his duties. William, the oldest son, had already followed his father's footsteps into the Navy, having become a midshipman the previous March. Glasgow stayed with his father, who, a little more than a year after Elizabeth's death, retired from the Navy to a 900-acre plantation on the Pascagoula River in Mississippi.

Some time after George Farragut moved to the plantation, David Porter Jr., a master commandant in the Navy who had arrived in New Orleans just five days before his father's death, paid George a visit. The younger Porter was a rising star in the

Navy. He had a flair for action, a willingness to take risks, and a keen tactical awareness. He was also impulsive, hotheaded, and keenly aware of his own personal honor. He became a midshipman in 1798, received his baptism of fire during the Quasi-War with France, fought pirates in the Caribbean, and battled Tripolitans in the Mediterranean during the Barbary Wars before arriving in New Orleans to command the naval station there.

Porter called on George Farragut because he had decided to take in one of George's children to repay the kindness Elizabeth had shown his father. Knowing Porter and his wife, Evalina, could give them a better home than he could, George agreed, provided Porter could convince one of the children to go. Porter noticed that eight-year-old Glasgow was smitten by the glittering brass buttons on his naval uniform. Porter promised to be the lad's "friend and guardian," and Glasgow volunteered to go. Porter took him back to New Orleans, where Mrs. Porter treated him as one of her own. Later in life, David Farragut remembered Porter "with feelings of the warmest gratitude." [2]

The Porters never adopted young Farragut, who continued to have a warm relationship with his father. Glasgow and his brothers frequently went sailing with George on Lake Pontchartrain. Neither afraid of danger nor fearful of exposing his children to it, George would take them out in all kinds of weather, and if darkness or storms prevented them from returning home, they would sleep on one of the islands wrapped up in the boat sails. Glasgow saw his father for the last time in 1810, when David Porter left New Orleans after his tour as commanding officer of the Naval Station there ended. [3]

Chapter 2

Baptism of Fire

IN JUNE 1810, the Porters and Glasgow embarked on a month-long voyage to Washington by way of Havana. The Porters spent several months in the capital, then went on to Mrs. Porter's home in Chester, Pennsylvania. Glasgow remained in Washington at school. Since the lad had voiced the ambition to become a naval officer like his father, brother, and guardian, Porter took him on a call to Secretary of the Navy Paul Hamilton. When Porter introduced Glasgow to the secretary as a boy who aspired to wear the uniform of an officer, Hamilton took the lad's hand and promised to appoint him a midshipman. The secretary was true to his word, and Farragut entered the Navy under a warrant dated December 17, 1810.

Early in August 1811, Midshipman Farragut accompanied Porter to Norfolk to join his guardian's new command, the 32-gun frigate *Essex*. Glasgow soon discovered that he was the youngest of the twelve midshipmen on board. The other young gentlemen doubtless teased Farragut and made him the butt of pranks, but they were quite taken with him, for he was talkative, friendly, and kind. A good joke aroused his mirth, while suffering aroused his sympathy. He loved to climb to the top of the mainmast, where he would sit and gaze out upon the sea. "Where's Glasgow?" Porter would ask when looking for the lad. "Up on the mainmast, sir," the quartermaster would reply, "looking for fresh air."[1]

Above all, Farragut was courageous. Not long after joining the *Essex,* Farragut was at a dock in Norfolk, performing his duty as midshipman of the captain's gig, nominally in charge of the boat's crew. While Farragut awaited Porter's return from whatever business the gig had taken him ashore to conduct, some rough-looking characters began to poke fun at him. Finally, one of them dumped the contents of an old water pot on the lad's head. A fight broke out instantly, with Farragut in the thick of it brandishing his dirk. The police intervened and arrested everyone, including the young midshipman. Rather than upsetting his guardian, however, Farragut's behavior pleased Porter, who is said to have remarked that the lad consisted of "three pounds of uniform and seventy pounds of fight."[2]

After a couple of post-refit shakedown cruises, the *Essex* wintered over at Newport, Rhode Island. At sea Farragut and the other midshipmen performed a variety of duties, such as echoing the orders of the officer of the deck and superintending the issue of provisions, water, and spirits to the men. Their primary responsibility, however, was to learn how to be naval officers. In March 1812 the *Essex* sailed for New York.

Three months later the United States declared war on Great Britain. For many years the British had been interfering with American merchant vessels and pressing American seamen into the Royal Navy in the course of fighting a series of wars against France. Finally the young nation had had enough. While other causes contributed, Americans went to war in 1812 largely to stop the British from trampling on their maritime commerce.

On July 3 the *Essex* put to sea in search of enemy ships. Porter soon found them. He captured six prizes and, on August 13, fought the war's first ship-to-ship engagement, defeating the 20-gun British sloop *Alert* with a single broadside. Farragut's first real achievement in the Navy came several nights later, when something startled him awake. It was an armed British sailor from one of the prizes, standing beside his hammock to see whether he and the other midshipmen were asleep. Farragut surmised instantly that a British plot was afoot to take the ship. He feigned sleep, realizing that he would be killed if he moved. Although he was quite afraid, when he was sure that the man was gone, he slipped quietly out of his hammock and crept to captain's cabin to report the incident in time for Porter to foil the plot. The cruise ended on September 15 when the *Essex* anchored at Chester, Pennsylvania.

For the next several weeks the *Essex's* crew prepared for what proved to be an epic voyage, unparalleled by that of any other American ship during the War of 1812. Late in October Farragut bade Mrs. Porter a tearful farewell and the *Essex* put to sea. Porter had originally intended to rendezvous with the fabled frigate *Constitution,* but when circumstances thwarted the plan, he made for the Pacific to destroy British commerce.

One day as the *Essex* sailed southward, Porter caught young Farragut chewing tobacco. The captain put his hand over the lad's mouth and made him swallow the quid. After this drastic cure Farragut never again used tobacco in any form.

When the *Essex* sailed across the equator, those among the crew who had not "crossed the line" before, including Farragut, were daubed with soap and tar, "shaved" with dull wooden "razors," and ducked in a tub of water in an age-old, grog-sodden maritime initiation ceremony in which they received the honored title "shellback."

After a stormy passage around Cape Horn and a stop in Valparaiso, Chile, the *Essex* roved through the Galapagos Islands, captured a dozen British whalers, and earned Porter the distinction of commanding the first American warship in the Pacific. During the voyage Farragut saw albatrosses, flying fish, seals, sea lions, redheaded lizards, iguanas, Galapagos terrapins, and other exotic wildlife. He also weathered fierce storms and choked down his share of worm- and weevil-ridden food.

When Porter had captured six British vessels, he decided to dispatch several to Valparaiso to sell them off. He fitted out one of the prizes as a warship, renamed her *Essex Junior,* and placed her under the command of Lieutenant John Downes to lead the detachment into port.

Extraordinarily, the twelve-year-old Farragut received command of another one of the prizes, the recaptured American whaler *Barclay.* The whaler's skipper and first mate remained on board to navigate. The skipper seethed with anger and resentment at the stoppage of his whaling, the prospect of losing his ship, and, worst of all, being placed under the command of a "damned nutshell," as he called Farragut. As the *Essex* sailed away and the detachment made for Valparaiso, the skipper tried to intimidate Farragut and regain control of his ship. After a heated exchange, the skipper stormed below to get his pistols. Although frightened, Farragut ordered the crew to make sail and close up with the *Essex Junior,* then sent word to the skipper that he would put him overboard if he came back up with his pistols. The skipper stayed below and Farragut remained in command, his action increasing the esteem in which everyone held him.

The detachment reached port only to find that Chile and Peru were at war, making it impossible to sell the prizes. Worse, Lieutenant Downes learned that the British frigate *Phoebe* and sloop *Cherub* were heading for the Pacific specifically to hunt down the *Essex.* Downes sent an oil-filled whaler to the United States, moored the other prizes in the harbor, and set sail with Farragut and the other prize-masters and crews in the *Essex Junior* to rejoin Porter in the Galapagos.

On October 25, 1813, the *Essex, Essex Junior,* and four captured vessels came into Nuku Hiva in the Marquesas, the easternmost islands of the Polynesian archipelagos. Despite the news of the British ships after him, Porter decided to careen and refit the *Essex* and to take time out for some "relaxation and amusement after being so long at sea," as he told the men. What followed could be grist for a Hollywood movie. One of the most beautiful islands in the Pacific, Nuku Hiva was a lush tropical paradise replete with palm trees, white sandy beaches, mountainous backdrops, and scantily clad natives. One contemporary writer noted that the "young girls" were "handsome and well-formed; their skins were remarkably soft and smooth, and their complexions no darker than many brunett[e]s in America."[3] The officers and men threw sexual repression to the wind and the situation soon became one of "helter-skelter and promiscuous intercourse, every girl the wife of every man," as Porter put it in his journal.[4] He spent nearly two months on the island, refitting and restocking his vessels and engaging in some of the island's endemic tribal warfare.

Farragut and the other young midshipmen remained under the close supervision of the chaplain, so they didn't get to do any of the fornicating or fighting, but Glasgow did spend many an afternoon rambling on shore with the native boys, who taught him how to swim better, throw a spear, and walk on stilts. With a great deal of sadness the crew of the *Essex* departed their tropical idyll on December 13 as a fiddler played "The Girl I Left Behind Me."

Porter should have carried his war against the British merchant marine into the Western Pacific and Indian Ocean and done his best to avoid the *Phoebe* and the *Cherub* but, blinded by an intemperate thirst for glory, he decided to seek out and engage the superior force. Porter brought the *Essex* and one of the captured vessels into Valparaiso on February 3, 1814, certain that the British vessels would appear there. Sure enough, they arrived five days later. Porter soon realized his mistake and determined to escape. While he was attempting to do so on March 28, a sudden gale tore away the *Essex's* main-topmast. His ship crippled, Porter tried to limp back into port, but the *Phoebe* and *Cherub* moved in for the kill and pounded the hapless American frigate with their longer-range guns.

During the battle Farragut served as captain's aide, quartergunner, and powder boy. He witnessed the evisceration of a boatswain's mate by one shot, the amputation of a quartermaster's leg by another, and the killing of four men by a third shot that splattered him with the last man's brains. He narrowly escaped death himself when a shot struck a man beside him full in the face. The man fell back on him, and the two tumbled down an open hatch, with the man landing on top of him. Farragut was bruised. The man's head was gone.

After two and a half hours of fighting, with 155 killed, wounded, or missing out of the ship's complement of 255, Porter ordered the colors struck. Farragut went below, where, as he recalled, he "became faint and sickened" at the sight of his wounded shipmates' mangled bodies. Porter included Farragut among those commended in his official report.

After the battle, Farragut went on board the *Phoebe,* where he spotted a British midshipman holding his pet pig. Farragut grabbed the pig, declaring that he would not give it up unless compelled to do so by force. The older British officers egged them on. A fight ensued. Farragut bested his British counterpart and delighted the bystanders.

In the days that followed, the British treated their American prisoners kindly and sent them home on the disarmed *Essex Junior.* The ship anchored off New York on July 7, just two days after Farragut's birthday. Barely thirteen, he had seen more of the world than most adults had at thirty, in his day or any other. A week later he went home to Chester, where he remained until the War of 1812 ended.

Chapter 3

Antebellum Naval Officer

N₀ SOONER DID one war end than Farragut headed for another. The Dey of Algiers had exploited U.S. preoccupation with the War of 1812 by preying on American commerce and demanding increased tribute. Tunis and Tripoli too had taken the opportunity to trample on American maritime rights. Congress declared war on March 15, 1815. The Navy dispatched two squadrons to the Mediterranean, one under Commodore Stephen Decatur and the other under Commodore William Bainbridge. Farragut served on board Bainbridge's flagship, the ship-of-the-line *Independence,* as aide to her skipper. Bainbridge arrived in midsummer, only to find that Decatur had already won all the battles and signed all the treaties. The *Independence* returned home that fall, arriving in Newport, Rhode Island, on November 15. Although denied another chance to distinguish himself in battle, Farragut benefited from the trip by befriending Midshipman William Taylor, an older lad who took him under his wing and served as a good role model.

After a brief stay in port and a month on board the frigate *Macedonian,* Farragut received orders on February 6, 1816 to the ship-of-the-line *Washington*. The big "liner," as such vessels were sometimes called, was flagship of the newly formed Mediterranean Squadron, which patrolled and defended American interests in that ancient and recurrently troubled sea. The *Washington* set sail in June and remained abroad for two years.

Farragut again served as aide to the skipper, a martinet obsessed with smartness, order, and cleanliness. Farragut was not impressed. "All this was accomplished at the sacrifice of the comfort of everyone on board," he recalled. "I determined never to have a 'crack ship,' if it was only to be attained by such means."[1]

The *Washington* routinely put in at exotic ports of call like Port Mahon on Minorca, Marseilles on the French Riviera, Naples on the Italian Peninsula, Messina and Syracuse on Sicily, and the Barbary ports of Tripoli, Tunis, and Algiers. Farragut had ample opportunity to sightsee and mingle with the families of diplomats and businessmen at various social calls, dinner parties, and balls. At Naples he saw Mount Vesuvius erupting and boiled eggs in a hot spring at the Baths of Nero. At a dinner party given by the head of the largest American business interest in Marseilles, Farragut was asked to play whist. Although he disliked cards, he sat in to be polite. The other players quickly grew impatient with his poor play and began making derisive comments. Finally one player got so fed up with Farragut that he threw his cards on the table. Farragut lost his temper and threw his own cards at the fellow's head. After regaining control of himself, he apologized to his host for behaving in such an ungentlemanly manner, then left.

During the cruise Farragut developed a keen interest in continuing his formal education. His urge to cultivate his mind and improve his already fine character impressed the chaplain and schoolmaster of the *Washington,* Charles Folsom. The two developed a close friendship. Farragut, seven years younger, looked upon the chaplain as an older brother. When Folsom was appointed American consul at Tunis, he arranged for Farragut to accompany him ashore to continue his education. Farragut was detached from the *Washington* in October 1817. He and Folsom arrived in Tunis in December.

Under the diplomat's tutelage, Farragut studied English literature, French, Italian, and mathematics. He also learned ancient history during innumerable walks and rides with Folsom along the Barbary coast. On one excursion, while examining the ruins of a Roman amphitheater outside Tunis, Farragut was confronted by a Bedouin swinging a club. Anticipating the character Indiana Jones by more than a century, Farragut drew two pistols from his pockets and trained them on his assailant. The Bedouin turned tail and fled. During another excursion, Farragut suffered a sunstroke that permanently weakened his vision and rendered him ever after unable to read or write more than a page at a time.

Before Farragut returned to sea, Folsom gave him a prophetic gift. It was a Turkish dagger, the scabbard of which was ornamented by an embossed scene representing a ship passing between the fire of two forts.

Farragut rejoined the squadron at Messina in February 1819, shipping on board the liner *Franklin*. The *Franklin* had become the flagship of the Mediterranean Squadron the previous summer when the *Washington* sailed for home. Farragut yet again served as aide to the skipper.

Impressed by Farragut's ability, knowledge, and deportment, the commodore of the Mediterranean Squadron ordered him to the brig *Spark* as an acting lieutenant in June 1819. Farragut considered this an honor, for he was only eighteen. He soon became the ship's executive officer. In the summer of 1820, he received orders to return to the United States and take the examination for promotion to lieutenant. Farragut booked passage on a merchant vessel bound for the United States by way of the Caribbean.

While sailing in the Caribbean, the skipper of the merchantman sighted a strange-looking craft, which he mistook for a pirate. Paralyzed with fear, he turned command of his ship over to Farragut. The skipper and his mates begged Farragut to remove his uniform, fearing that it would incite the pirates to violence. But Farragut refused and inspired the crew to prepare for battle. The strange vessel turned out to be a Colombian brig, not a pirate, so no fight materialized. But once again, Farragut had seen determination and action counteract fear and panic. The merchantman reached the United States shortly thereafter.

Farragut arrived in Washington in September and reported himself ready for the examination. While taking it, he made the mistake of arguing with one of the examiners. He realized the error too late and left the room with tears in his eyes. The examiners failed him. "It was the hardest blow I have ever sustained to my pride and the greatest mortification to my vanity," Farragut later recalled.[2] After several months leave, in January 1821 Farragut received orders for duty ashore at Norfolk. He retook the exam there in October and passed it this time, standing twentieth out of fifty-three. In those days promotion to lieutenant was not immediately forthcoming, so Farragut languished as a "passed midshipman" for over three more years. Meanwhile, he longed to return to sea and, after repeated application for duty afloat, finally received orders to the frigate *John Adams* in May 1822. Three months later the *John Adams* departed Norfolk for a five-month cruise in the Gulf of Mexico, during which Farragut dined one evening at Vera Cruz with future Mexican dictator Antonio Lopez de Santa Anna.

Shortly after the *John Adams* returned to Norfolk, Farragut learned that Commodore David Porter had been given command of the West India Squadron and would soon set sail for the Caribbean to hunt pirates. This kind of duty appealed to Farragut, so his old friend and patron had him reassigned under his command.

Piracy had plagued the Caribbean since the sixteenth century, remittent but always present. One expert had cataloged exactly 3,002 "piratical acts" committed in those waters between 1815 and 1822, many involving unspeakable cruelty.

Porter's "Mosquito Fleet" of three sloops, eleven schooners, five 20-oared barges, a storeship, and the *Sea Gull,* the first sidewheel steamer ever to engage in naval hostilities, departed wintry Norfolk in February 1823 for the sunny Caribbean. Generally speaking, Porter's squadron struck piracy a serious blow in the region but, lacking the cooperation of local governments, failed to eradicate it.

Farragut sailed in one of the schooners, the *Greyhound*. On one occasion he led a shore party in cleaning out a nest of pirates near the southeast point of Cuba. That summer Farragut's brother William, then a lieutenant, joined the squadron and served briefly with Glasgow on board the *Greyhound*. It was the first time they had seen each other since Glasgow had left New Orleans with Porter thirteen years earlier. In August Porter transferred Glasgow Farragut to the *Sea Gull*.

Farragut remained in the Caribbean on the steamer until May 1824, when he secured a leave of absence to see his relatives in New Orleans. His ten-day visit with his sister Nancy was one of the happiest times of his life, but the reunion turned bittersweet when they reminisced about their parents and youngest brother, all of whom were now dead. Glasgow didn't get the opportunity to see his other sister, Elizabeth, who lived in Pascagoula.

After the visit Farragut returned to duty at Key West, where he was placed in command of the schooner *Ferret*. With Porter's squadron having driven the pirates into hiding, Farragut had to content himself with escorting merchantmen and other prosaic duties until he was stricken with yellow fever that July. He spent August convalescing in Washington, then went to Norfolk to marry his sweetheart, Susan Caroline Marchant.

Glasgow had met Susan in Norfolk after he had failed the lieutenant's exam. "The consolation of a charming young lady, who smiled on my attentions," he later recalled, softened the blow.[3] Since then he had courted her whenever fate brought him to Norfolk, which he now considered home. The wedding took place at Trinity Church in Portsmouth, Virginia, on September 2, 1824.

Farragut spent the next several months enjoying married life and finishing his convalescence. He was finally promoted to lieutenant in January 1825. In August he received orders to the beautiful new frigate *Brandywine*, under the command of Captain

Charles Morris, a hero of the Barbary Wars and the War of 1812. The *Brandywine* had been so named to honor a hero of the Revolution, the marquis de Lafayette, who was wounded at the battle of Brandywine Creek. The frigate was to transport Lafayette home to France at the end of his triumphal tour of the United States in 1824 and 1825. She set sail in September 1825, reaching Le Havre after a relatively short voyage of nearly a month. The crew gave Lafayette a major general's salute as the sixty-eight-year-old hero left the ship. The *Brandywine* wintered at Port Mahon, then set sail for New York, arriving there in April 1826.

The next month an official errand brought Farragut home to Norfolk, where he found Susan ill with neuralgia. He requested and was granted leave of absence to care for her. They summered in New Haven, Connecticut, with Glasgow attending lectures at Yale and Susan under the care of one of the nation's best physicians. Even so, her health worsened. They returned to Norfolk that fall. In November Farragut was ordered to the receiving ship *Alert,* whose skipper allowed Susan to live on board so Glasgow could better care for her. Farragut remained in Norfolk for two years, during which he established on the *Alert* a school for training apprentice seamen.

In October 1828, Farragut received orders to the sloop *Vandalia* for a cruise on the Brazil Station. The ship sailed two months later, arriving at Rio de Janeiro in February 1829. Farragut remained with the *Vandalia* in South American waters until deteriorating vision obliged him to return home. During these years Farragut suffered from bouts of seasickness. Many a time when serving as officer of the deck, he had to stop in the middle of giving an order, lean over the side, and "pay tribute to Neptune."

Farragut arrived in Norfolk in February 1830 only to find his wife bedridden. He remained in Norfolk and served on receiving ships until the summer of 1832, when he was granted leave to seek medical treatment for Susan in Philadelphia. After she got a little better, Farragut reported himself ready for duty and in December received orders to the sloop *Natchez* as first lieutenant.

In January 1833 the sloop sailed for Charleston as part of President Andrew Jackson's demonstration of Federal authority during the crisis that arose when South Carolina adopted an ordinance of nullification that repudiated the tariff acts of 1828 and 1832. In March 1833, Henry Clay forged a compromise between President Jackson and nullification leader John C. Calhoun that, for the time being, preserved the Union. Farragut, serving on board a U.S. warship at the very center of the controversy during its most dangerous phase, fully understood both sides' arguments and fully supported the Federal position. The *Natchez* returned to Norfolk the next month.

After a short leave, Farragut embarked on the *Natchez* in May for a voyage back to the Brazil Station. There he continued serving as first lieutenant until March 1834, when he became skipper of the schooner *Boxer,* his second command. He remained in South American waters until the *Boxer* was ordered home. Farragut brought her into Norfolk in July.

With the Navy then in one of its periodic "dark ages" and many more officers available than berths on warships, Farragut spent nearly four years in Norfolk awaiting orders. Finally, in March 1838, he was directed to report to Pensacola, Florida, for duty on the West India Station. He arrived there a month later and shipped on board the frigate *Constellation.*

In August the commodore placed Farragut in command of the sloop *Erie,* his third command and best to date. For five months he cruised in the Gulf of Mexico between Tampico and Vera Cruz, where on November 27 he witnessed a French naval squadron in action at San Juan de Ulloa. When a naval blockade failed to compel the Mexican government to pay claims for damages inflicted on French citizens living in Mexico, the French squadron reduced the fortress there in a five-and-a-half-hour bombardment.

The result flew in the face of the conventional wisdom that naval forces unsupported by ground forces could not reduce forts. The Duke of Wellington remarked that it was the only example known to him of a strong fort falling to sea power alone. A new kind of naval ordnance secured the victory—shell guns developed by one of Napoleon's artillery officers, Henri Joseph

Paixhans, and adopted by the French navy only a year earlier. During the bombardment French ships fired more than 7,700 solid shot and not quite 200 shells. While the shot embedded themselves in the fort's soft limestone walls without doing much damage, the shells penetrated and then exploded, tearing out large chunks of stone.

Farragut visited the fort shortly after its surrender. The performance of the new ordnance so impressed him that he filed a report with the commodore of the West India Squadron, declaring that while the French navy had made significant progress in ordnance since their last war with England, "we are standing still."[4] Indeed, the French development of shell guns, coupled with the development of steam propulsion, revolutionized naval warfare during the nineteenth century. The rest of the cruise passed uneventfully. Farragut brought the *Erie* back to Pensacola in January 1839, visited briefly with his sister Nancy in New Orleans, then returned to Norfolk.

That same month Farragut published an account of the French operations at Vera Cruz in the New Orleans *Commercial Bulletin*. The French admiral in charge objected vehemently to the account, calling Farragut a "grave liar." The secretary of the navy reprimanded Farragut for questioning the conduct of "an officer of a foreign Government with which we are at peace." The issue wasn't whether Farragut's account was accurate, which it was, but the "impropriety" of publishing it under an official signature. The secretary's ire eventually subsided, but he kept Farragut awaiting orders for two years.[5]

Farragut spent most of the time in Norfolk nursing his invalid wife. He did everything he could to relieve her suffering, but to no avail. Toward the end she became so weak and helpless that he had "to lift her and carry her about like a child," as he later recalled.[6] Finally, after struggling against illness for sixteen years, Susan Caroline Marchant Farragut died on December 27, 1840. Farragut's tender devotion to Susan throughout her illness deeply impressed the ladies of Norfolk. "When Captain Farragut dies," one of them remarked, "he should have a monument reaching to the skies, made by every wife in the city contributing a stone to it."[7]

After Susan's funeral, Farragut applied for sea duty. He received orders to the ship-of-the-line *Delaware* as executive officer in February 1841. On September 27, he was promoted to commander. After an overhaul and stops at Annapolis and Norfolk, the *Delaware* set sail for the Brazil Station in November. In June 1842, Farragut took command of the sloop *Decatur,* which cruised on the Brazil Station until returning to Norfolk in February 1843.

With no orders for active duty immediately forthcoming, Farragut took a leave of absence and spent the summer at Fauquier Springs, Virginia. There he met and fell in love with Virginia Dorcas Loyall of Norfolk. The two got married in Norfolk on December 26, 1843.

In April 1844, Farragut received orders as executive officer to the ship-of-the-line *Pennsylvania,* the biggest sailing warship ever built for the U.S. Navy, then relegated to serving as a receiving ship at Norfolk. On October 12, Virginia bore Farragut their only child, a son whom they named Loyall. The child spent his infancy in his father's cabin on board the *Pennsylvania.* Farragut remained in Norfolk until March 1847, when he received command of the sloop *Saratoga.*

Farragut had been chomping at the bit for a command afloat in the Gulf of Mexico even before the Mexican War broke out in the spring of 1846. Several months after hostilities commenced, he presented to the secretary of the navy a plan for taking the fort at San Juan de Ulloa. If the secretary intended to mount an expedition against the fort, Farragut declared, he hoped to take part. The secretary listened politely, but dismissed the plan as visionary and impracticable. Its daring, however, impressed a bureau chief named Gideon Welles. An uncannily good judge of character, Welles would remember the plan and the bold officer who presented it when he became Abraham Lincoln's secretary of the navy.

Farragut never got the chance to distinguish himself during the Mexican War, for the *Saratoga* didn't arrive off Vera Cruz until April 1847, days after the city had surrendered to American forces under Major General Winfield Scott. Instead of winning a glorious victory, Farragut came down with yellow fever and nearly died. But he recovered and performed blockade duty until ordered to New York, where he arrived in February 1848.

Farragut spent the next two years ashore as second-in-command of the Norfolk Navy Yard. During this tour he was stricken with cholera, but got better after several weeks of recuperation in White Sulfur Springs. Relieved of duty at the navy yard in May 1850, he took his family to the mountains in Botetourt County, Virginia for the summer.

When he returned to duty, the navy put him to work on a series of ordnance assignments. In October 1850, he headed up a board convened in part to evaluate some of the inventions recently sprung from the fertile mind of Lieutenant John A. Dahlgren, who had been tinkering with ordnance at the Washington Navy Yard since 1847 and who would go down in history as "the father of American naval ordnance" for his contributions. Farragut and Dahlgren locked horns over a firing lock that Dahlgren claimed to have invented but which Farragut attributed to another inventor.

The two locked horns again over Dahlgren's idea for a new system of ordnance. The war with Mexico had revealed the need for a weapon light enough to mount in boats for use in shallow waters in support of amphibious landings and forces ashore. Dahlgren had invented a nifty little bronze boat gun to do just that. He had also designed a boat carriage and a field carriage for the gun. In an amphibious assault, the gun could be fired rapidly from the boat carriage during the approach to shore, then transferred quickly to the field carriage once the boat landed. Farragut practiced with the boat gun in simulated amphibious operations, but preferred to use the field carriage in the boat to save time otherwise spent in transferring the gun between carriages. Dahlgren found the field carriage to be unstable in boats, and since the gun bore his name and not Farragut's, the Navy adopted both carriages. In all, Farragut spent six months in charge of the ordnance board.

Beginning in March 1851, Farragut spent eighteen months in Washington drawing up a book of ordnance regulations for the Navy. Then he returned to the Norfolk Navy Yard in April 1852 to give weekly lectures on ordnance to the officers stationed there. The following August he was ordered to Fort Monroe, across Hampton Roads from Norfolk, to test the endurance of every type of gun in the Navy, along with a new type of cannon whose peculiar shape reminded him of a soda-water bottle. The queer-looking cannon, a big, heavy, 9-incher, was the prototype of a new kind of ordnance with which the ambitious Dahlgren hoped to rearm the entire fleet.

For month after month, Farragut fired round after round from each gun until it burst from the strain, seeking to determine whether the density and tensile strength of metal in a cannon had any correlation to its endurance. Lieutenant Percival Drayton, who was to be Farragut's fleet captain during the battle of Mobile Bay, worked with him during the last six weeks of the experiments. Drayton found him to be "an energetic fellow full of zeal."[8]

The prototype Dahlgren gun turned in an impressive performance, withstanding nearly a thousand rounds in a day when naval cannons were only expected to endure five hundred. Even so, Farragut didn't like the 9-incher as much as he did the lighter 8-inch shell gun, again to Dahlgren's dismay. But once again Dahlgren prevailed in the feud over ordnance ideas with Farragut, for Dahlgren's soda-water bottle guns and boat guns would soon become the Navy's standard armament. Nevertheless, the endurance tests and the opportunity to work with the boat guns and 9-incher almost at the ground floor of their development gave Farragut a finer appreciation for what the Navy's tools of war could do than most naval officers got in their entire career. In August 1853 Farragut completed the endurance experiments and resumed the weekly lectures at the Norfolk Navy Yard.

When England and France joined Turkey against Russia in the Crimean War the following spring, Farragut wanted the Navy Department to send him overseas to see how the latest European ordnance would fare in combat. Instead the department sent him to California to establish a navy yard at Mare Island. After a bout of illness, Farragut, along with Virginia and Loyall, embarked in August 1854 on a steamer bound for Nicaragua, where they arrived after a ten-day passage. Then came a difficult journey across Nicaragua by steamboat and wagon, after which the family took a steamer to San Fransciso, where they arrived in mid-September.

Farragut officially took command of Mare Island on the sixteenth. After running off squatters, he superintended the construction of shops, quarters, docks, and repair facilities, developing a good rapport with the workmen under his charge. The invigorating northern California climate along with daily horseback rides did wonders for his health, which for thirty years had suffered under recurrent attacks of yellow fever and other illnesses. In the fall of 1855, Farragut received a commission as captain, then the navy's highest rank. In order of seniority, he stood thirty-ninth on the list of eighty-one captains. When the construction ended and the navy yard opened for business, Farragut remained at Mare Island as commandant until the summer of 1858, then returned to New York by way of Panama. Building and running the Mare Island Navy Yard gave him valuable logistics and management experience.

After arriving in New York, Farragut took Virginia and Loyall to Poughkeepsie for the fall. When all the leaves had come down, the family went home to Norfolk in December. They had no sooner arrived when Farragut received orders to go back to New York to take command of the steam sloop *Brooklyn*.

The *Brooklyn* symbolized the Navy's antebellum renaissance. Endeavors across a broad spectrum of fields over the past twenty years had fundamentally changed the Navy. Reorganization of naval administration into the bureau system in 1842, the founding of the Naval Academy in 1845, and a clumsy attempt to cull the deadwood out of the officer corps in 1855 represented a growing professionalization of the officer corps. Various ocean exploration expeditions and Matthew Fontaine Maury's pioneering work in charting ocean winds and currents placed American naval officers at the forefront of nineteenth-century science. The opening of Japan to foreign trade resulting from Matthew C. Perry's expeditions to that country in 1853 and 1854 transcended normal naval diplomacy.

Naval technology was undergoing a revolution. The work of Dahlgren and various European ordnance experts, featuring the application of scientific methods and theories and systematic research and development, produced shell guns and later rifled cannons that precipitated the construction of armored warships.

But more than any other single development, it was the introduction of steam propulsion that sparked the nineteenth-century naval revolution. After a few fits and false starts, steam propulsion took root in the U.S. Navy in the late 1830s. What came to be called the steam navy really came into its own when congress authorized the *Merrimack*-class frigates in 1854 and five steam sloops in 1857.

The *Brooklyn,* the first of these sloops off the ways, represented the state of the art in warship technology. Larger than the average ship-of-the-line during the age of sail, she displaced 2,532 tons and stretched 233 feet along the waterline. She carried a full ship rig for sailing, a propeller fourteen and a half feet in diameter driven by two horizontal direct-acting, crosshead engines for steaming, and a battery of two boat guns, one 10-inch pivot gun, and twenty 9-inch Dahlgren guns for fighting. The *Brooklyn* was one of the Navy's most powerful warships, and it was an honor for Farragut to command her.

In February 1859 Farragut took the *Brooklyn* for a trial run down to Beaufort, South Carolina, then on a cruise in the Caribbean. Except for occasional forays back to the United States for supplies, to run diplomatic errands, and to attend a trial arising from the death of one of his crewmen, Farragut remained in the Caribbean on the *Brooklyn* until October 1860.

One of Farragut's errands involved taking a diplomat to Vera Cruz through rough weather. "I can't help loving my profession," he noted of the voyage, "but it has materially changed since the advent of steam. I took as much pleasure in running into this port the other day in a gale of wind as ever a boy did in any feat of skill." Even after nearly fifty years in the Navy, his enthusiasm for the sea remained as fresh as it had been when as a boy he would climb up the mainmast "looking for fresh air." [9]

Exercises with the *Brooklyn's* battery during the cruise led Farragut to reiterate his preference for the old 8-inch shell gun over Dahlgren's new 9-incher in a report to the chief of the Bureau of Ordnance and Hydrography. Dahlgren felt that Farragut "as usual got the cart before the horse," but Farragut believed that gunnery depended as much on the "eye and practice of the Gunner" as on the gun itself. [10]

After leaving the *Brooklyn,* Farragut returned to the United States. He wintered in Poughkeepsie, where Loyall was attending the Dutchess County Academy, then went home to Norfolk, cooling his heels while awaiting orders.

Chapter 4

Triumph at New Orleans

MEANWHILE, THE COUNTRY came apart. The Compromise of 1850, the emergence of the Republican party, "bleeding Kansas," the Dred Scott case, and John Brown's raid on Harper's Ferry had driven wedges of separation between the North and the South. However you boil it down, at bottom lay the issue of slavery, with Northerners seeking to contain the "peculiar institution" and Southerners seeking its expansion. The split came after the election of "Honest Old Abe Lincoln, the Railsplitter," in November 1860. Fearing that the "Black Republicans" meant to do away with slavery altogether, South Carolina, Mississippi, Florida, Alabama, Georgia, Louisiana, and Texas seceded from the Union and, on February 4, 1861, formed their own government, which they dubbed the Confederate States of America. The Republican president's inauguration, the Rebel attack on Fort Sumter, and Lincoln's call to arms and proclamation of a blockade of southern ports precipitated the departure from the Union of Virginia, Arkansas, North Carolina, and Tennessee, all of whom joined the Confederacy as well.

Although Farragut had been born and raised in the South and

now made his home in Norfolk, he never wavered in his loyalty to the Union. For fifty years he had served afloat and ashore under the flag of the United States, and it was to that flag that he felt he owed his allegiance, not to any state. Nearly thirty years earlier he had served on a warship representing Federal authority in Charleston during the nullification crisis and had stood ready to preserve the Union by force. He had observed the horrors of civil war during revolutions in Latin American countries during tours of duty on the Brazil and West India Stations. The prospect of "fighting our own people," as he later put it, tormented him during many sleepless nights.[1] Early in the secession crisis, he figured that if the North and South parted amicably, he would settle among family and friends in Norfolk. But if it came to war, and war seemed increasingly inevitable, he intended to serve the federal government as he always had. The question of slavery didn't seem to factor into his figuring.[2]

Throughout the crisis, leading citizens of Norfolk and naval officers stationed there met regularly at a certain store to discuss the political situation, no doubt surrounding a potbellied stove as they talked. When Farragut spoke of the evils of civil war toward which the country seemed to be drifting, the others called him "croaker" and "granny." When the Virginia state convention passed the ordinance of secession on April 17, the citizens of Norfolk took to the streets, cheering and firing guns while the militia paraded about playing music and flying Southern flags.

Farragut went to the store the next morning, distraught by what had happened. The other naval officers, most of them Southerners, treated him coolly. Most of them had already resigned in preparation to "go South" to serve the Confederacy. When Farragut said that Lincoln was fully justified in calling for troops in the wake of Southern seizures of forts and arsenals, a former brother officer told him bluntly that since Virginia had seceded, he needed to resign himself or get out of Norfolk.

In his heart Farragut knew the fellow was right, for he had no desire to be called to duty to the Norfolk Navy Yard and perhaps be compelled to fight against friends and relatives from town. He hastened home and announced to Virginia that he was "sticking to the flag." "This act of mine may cause years of separation from your family," he told her, "so you must decide quickly whether you will go North or remain here."³ Virginia decided to follow her husband.

The Farraguts gathered their prized possessions, bade Virginia's family a tearful farewell, and went down to the wharf amid dirty looks and mumbled threats from onlookers. They got there safely, boarded a steamer, and arrived in Baltimore on April 19, not long after a mob had attacked Massachusetts troops passing through on their way to Washington and one day before an elderly, alcoholic officer abandoned the Norfolk Navy Yard to the Rebels. From Baltimore they traveled to Hastings-on-Hudson, some fifteen miles upstream from New York City, where Farragut rented a house, settled the family, and wrote to Gideon Welles, whom Lincoln had recently appointed Secretary of the Navy, to explain why he had left Norfolk. He then awaited orders.

The waiting dragged on for months. At first, some of the citizens of Hastings looked askance at the Southern-born newcomer, who often took long walks in the hills surrounding the village. Gossip had it that he was actually a Confederate agent who spent his ramblings concocting a scheme to destroy the Croton Aqueduct, which carried water to New York City.

But even the worst suspicions soon evaporated as the neighbors got to know the genial, athletic old man. Farragut stood five feet, six and a half inches tall and weighed 150 pounds. His fondness for exercise gave him a trim figure for a man of sixty, but the deep lines and leathery skin on his face and his thinning, graying hair clearly showed his age. Those who got to know him well found him an excellent host and conversationalist, with a ready smile, gentlemanly manners, good humor, and a clever way with words.

While Farragut waited, the Navy made preparations to enforce the blockade, mount combined operations with the Army to capture strategic points on the Southern coast and along the Mississippi River, and hunt down Rebel commerce raiders and privateers operating on the high seas. The preparations largely involved acquiring and building ships and finding and training crews to man them.

Farragut must have wondered why he hadn't been called to duty during the summer of 1861. There were two reasons. Early in the war the Navy had more high-ranking officers than ships for them to command. But more important, Secretary Welles remained wary of naval officers born in the South, for good reason. In the spring of 1861, the U.S. Navy had 571 lieutenants, commanders, and captains, of whom 253 (44 percent) were Southern born. Of these 253, half (126) resigned to go South. While Farragut never considered resigning, his background understandably made the Navy Department a tad cautious.

Farragut's leaving Norfolk and settling in upstate New York had done much to allay such suspicions, however, and in September, Gideon Welles ordered him to the Brooklyn Navy Yard to serve on a board convened to recommend officers for retirement from active duty. The task demanded the utmost tact, wisdom, and impartiality. Farragut found the daily grind of old commodores and medical officers droning on about dropping some poor devil from the service maddeningly dull. To break up the monotony, he visited shipyards around New York where men-of-war were abuilding. He looked askance at a new type of vessel whose keel was laid on October 25 at Green Point, Long Island. The ship, named the *Monitor,* was destined to herald the nineteenth-century naval revolution that doomed wooden-walled warships. Farragut wasn't impressed.

Meanwhile, plans were afoot in Washington that would give Farragut a chance for action beyond his wildest dreams. One of the Lincoln administration's central strategic objectives was to gain control of the Mississippi River. Early debate raged about whether to start in Cairo, Illinois, and campaign downstream or to start at the mouth of the river and campaign upstream. Ultimately it would be both.

Either way, the prize would be New Orleans. In the half century since Farragut had left there with David Porter, New

Orleans had become the richest city in the South and the second largest port in the antebellum United States, with a population numbering nearly 170,000. While the Crescent City still served as a conduit for midwestern farm products as it had during Farragut's childhood, cotton was now king, accounting for 60 percent of port receipts in 1860. It was the advent of the steamboat that had made it all possible. Steamboats carried goods and passengers reasonably on schedule, upriver as well as down, making New Orleans the principal entrepôt between Mississippi River and overseas trade. Thus blessed with abundant economic opportunities, the Crescent City attracted a distinctly unsouthern population of foreigners, mechanics, manufacturers, merchants, shipbuilders, and capitalists. Nevertheless, geography, king cotton, and strong pro-slavery sentiment wedded it to the Confederacy.

New Orleans' principal defenses to the south consisted of a pair of forts lying astride the Mississippi at a point seventy river miles below the city and twenty river miles above the river's mouth. The first fort that ships coming upriver from the Gulf would encounter was Fort Jackson, standing one hundred yards from the levee on the west bank of the Mississippi. Fort Jackson was a star-shaped work of stone and mortar with 22-foot-high walls and mounting seventy-four guns. A line of obstructions ran from a point abreast Fort Jackson seven hundred yards across the river to the opposite shore. A half mile upstream on the opposite bank stood Fort St. Philip, a sod-covered brick and stone structure mounting fifty-two guns. Some eleven hundred men garrisoned the two forts.

The plan for the capture of New Orleans taking shape in the Navy Department envisioned a purely naval attack. Although powerful defensive works, Forts Jackson and St. Philip depended upon New Orleans for supplies that, because of the marshes surrounding their land faces, could only come by river. A fleet anchored above the forts would cut their line of communications, rendering their fall only a matter of time. In broad outline, the plan entailed running a fleet past the forts, seizing their base—New Orleans—then turning the city over to Army occupation troops.

Who first hatched the idea of passing the forts is shrouded by the mists of time and postwar jockeying for the credit. What is clear is that on November 15, 1861, President Lincoln, Secretary Welles, Assistant Secretary of the Navy Gustavus Fox, and a 47-year-old Navy commander fresh from blockade duty at the mouth of the Mississippi met in the home of Major General George B. McClellan, who had become general-in-chief of the Union army two weeks earlier, to discuss the capture of New Orleans. That commander was none other than David Dixon Porter, the son of Farragut's guardian David Porter. Although David Dixon Porter and Farragut hadn't seen much of each other growing up, they regarded one another as brothers. Porter argued that wooden ships couldn't pass the forts unless the forts were reduced first. A flotilla of bomb boats firing Army mortars, he declared, could do the job in two days. Fox objected strenuously to a preliminary bombardment, but Welles and McClellan liked the idea, the latter probably because it would ensure Army participation in what would be a glorious operation, if it succeeded. In the end the Navy Department adopted the plan, including the mortar boats. Welles placed Porter in command of the mortar flotilla, then tackled the much more difficult problem of choosing a commander to lead the expedition.

The mists of time and postwar scrambling for credit also obscure who first proposed Farragut to lead the expedition, but final authority for appointing the commander rested with the secretary of the navy. The officer in charge in the Gulf, Flag Officer William W. McKean, was ill and needed to be replaced. Welles went down the list of officers in order of seniority, ruling out several not already assigned to a command for various reasons. When he came to Farragut, Welles recalled being impressed by his decision to clear out of Norfolk when Virginia seceded. He also remembered Farragut's bold but carefully crafted plan to take the fort at San Juan de Ulloa.

Welles then polled the Navy's senior leaders about Farragut.

"All who knew him gave him the credit of being a good officer of good sense and good habits," the secretary recalled after the war, "who had faithfully and correctly discharged his duty in every position to which he had been assigned." Farragut "had a good but not a conspicuous record" and had never commanded a squadron before.[4] Yet he was one of the few officers with sufficient rank to command a squadron who also had the strength and vigor necessary to bear the strain of arduous duty.

Welles summoned Farragut to Washington for an interview. Farragut met Fox for breakfast at the home of Postmaster General Montgomery Blair on December 21. When Fox laid out the plan for the attack on New Orleans, Farragut said that it was certain to succeed. After breakfast Farragut went to Welles's office, where he reiterated his approval of the plan. He expressed doubt about the utility of the mortars, but agreed to give them a try. Welles offered him command of the expedition, and Farragut accepted. "I expect to pass the forts and restore New Orleans to the Government, or never return," he declared in a rush of enthusiasm. "I may not come back, but the city will be ours."[5]

After the meeting Farragut went home to put his affairs in order, then returned to Washington to begin preparations for the expedition to New Orleans. His official appointment to command the West Gulf Blockading Squadron arrived in January 1862. With the appointment came responsibility for enforcing the blockade from the mouth of the Rio Grande to St. Andrew's Bay in Florida as well as leading the attack on New Orleans.

Farragut then went to the Philadelphia Navy Yard to meet his flagship, the USS *Hartford*. The third of the 1857 sloops off the ways, the *Hartford* closely resembled the *Brooklyn*. Farragut beefed up her armament and had quarter-inch rims of boiler iron installed around her fore and main tops. The *Hartford* stood to sea on January 25 and four days later arrived at Hampton Roads. There Farragut received orders to take possession of New Orleans, push up the Mississippi River, reduce the forts defending Mobile Bay, and blockade the coast within his area of responsibility.

Concern for his men topped Farragut's agenda. "My greatest anxiety now," he wrote Gus Fox on January 30, "is to have proper comforts for the sick and wounded, for somebody will be hurt." Before continuing the voyage south Farragut requisitioned one hundred iron bedsteads and arranged to convert one of his vessels into a hospital ship "with every facility for getting the men on board without torment." He took pains to stock a large supply of tourniquets. "More men lose their lives by bleeding to death from want of early attention," he noted, "than from the severity of the wounds." "It is a great gratification to *Jack* to see that his comforts are looked to, when he is sick," he added.[6]

The *Hartford* put to sea again on February 2. After stopping briefly at Port Royal, Key West, and Havana, she reached Ship Island on February 20. Ship Island, a low sandbank nearly devoid of vegetation and so named because its shape suggested that of a ship with her bow pointed toward New Orleans, lay some thirty miles south of Biloxi, Mississippi. The Navy had occupied the island in September 1861 and had been using it as a base ever since. Upon his arrival there, Farragut officially took command of the West Gulf Blockading Squadron.

In the coming weeks Farragut's squadron grew to forty-three warships, including twenty mortar schooners and six gunboats under Porter. Farragut's principal strength lay in his eight steam sloops, five of which mounted more than twenty guns apiece, and nine gunboats mounting four or five guns apiece. In all, Farragut's ships carried 182 guns. Porter's twenty mortar schooners each mounted a 13-inch mortar and two guns, while his gunboats carried a total of twenty-seven guns. The Army contributed some twelve thousand troops under Major General Benjamin F. Butler, detailed to participate in combined operations against New Orleans, Vicksburg, and Mobile. Butler's plan for New Orleans, as Farragut put it, was simply "to follow in my wake and hold what I can take."[7]

In addition to Forts Jackson and St. Philip, the Rebels mustered six armed tugs with iron-reinforced prows for ramming; four gunboats; two launches; the ironclad ram *Manassas;* and two unfinished ironclads, the *Mississippi* and the *Louisiana.* In all these vessels mounted forty guns: sixteen on the *Louisiana,* eight on the gunboat *McRae,* and one or two on each of the rest. The Rebels also prepared numerous fire rafts, piling wood saturated with tar and turpentine into immense flatboats, to unleash on ships attacking from downriver.

Unfortunately for the Rebel cause, Confederate President Jefferson Davis and Secretary of the Navy Stephen R. Mallory believed that the principal danger to the Confederacy lay upriver. A fleet of armored Union gunboats under Flag Officer Andrew Hull Foote in combined operations with the U.S. Army had captured Fort Henry on the Tennessee River on February 6, Fort Donelson on the Cumberland River on February 16, and Island No. 10 in the upper Mississippi on April 7. To try to stop this juggernaut, Davis and Mallory stripped New Orleans of troops and sent a large portion of the Confederate river fleet to Memphis.

Mallory had also been lax in pushing for completion of the *Mississippi* and the *Louisiana,* which had the potential to be the most formidable vessels on the river, but not until their armor and engines were installed. Now the Confederates raced to finish them before Farragut launched his attack. Without the ironclads, Forts Jackson and St. Philip constituted New Orleans' best hope for staving off the impending onslaught.

Early in March, Farragut issued a detailed general order to his skippers on how to ready their ships for service in the river. Excess spars, rigging, and masts were to be taken down and landed. As many guns as possible were to be placed for firing ahead and astern against enemy vessels and shore batteries, as it would be difficult to maneuver in the current for firing broadsides. Grapnels and boats were to be readied for towing off fire rafts. Each vessel was to be trimmed a few inches by the head, so that if she touched bottom, she would not swing head downstream. If a ship's machinery was damaged, she was to back downriver.

The order emphasized the importance of damage control:

> You will see that force and other pumps and engine hose are in good order, and men stationed by them, and your men will be drilled to the extinguishing of fire.
>
> Have light Jacob ladders made to throw over the side for the use

of the carpenters in stopping shot holes, who are to be supplied with pieces of inch board lined with felt, and ordinary nails. . . . Have many tubs of water about the decks, both for the purpose of extinguishing fire and for drinking. . . . I expect every vessel's crew to be well exercised at their guns, because it is required by the regulations of the service, and is usually the first object of our attention, but they must be equally well trained for stopping shot holes and extinguishing fire. Hot and cold shot will no doubt be freely dealt to us, and there must be stout hearts and quick hands to extinguish the one and stop the holes of the other. [8]

Farragut considered damage control every bit as important as gunnery.

He spent the following weeks beefing up the repair and supply facilities on Ship Island, getting the deeper-draft ships over the bar into the Mississippi, and making preparations for the attack. He waded through a seemingly endless stream of paperwork dealing with coal, food, ammunition, boilers, machinery, and a thousand other details, his clerks reading aloud to him when his weak eyes prevented him from reading for himself.

Meanwhile, Farragut gathered every scrap of information he could on the enemy's defenses. He pored over dispatches from Washington enumerating Rebel naval forces at New Orleans, warning of ironclads abuilding at New Orleans and Mobile, enclosing sketches of the defenses along the lower Mississippi by Army engineers, and containing detailed information on Forts Jackson and St. Philip by an officer who had worked on them before the war. He read letters and papers from captured blockade runners and reports of prisoner interrogations. He listened to reports of officers whom he had sent upriver on reconnaissance missions. He dispatched officers to take soundings as far up the river and deep into the surrounding bayous as possible.

On April 5, Farragut embarked on the sloop *Iroquois* and steamed upriver with four other gunboats to see the Confederate defenses for himself. When the ships came within sight of the forts and obstructions, the Confederates opened fire. To the sailors' amusement, several of the officers on the quarterdeck ducked and bobbed and dodged with each shot. But not Farragut. He stood rock steady on the horse block, glass in hand, commenting on the Rebel gunnery. "There comes one!" he cried. "There! There!!" The shot fell short, splashing in the water. "Ah, too short," Farragut said. "Finely lined though!" [9]

The intelligence that Farragut gathered gave him an incomplete and inaccurate picture of his foe. A report from Washington indicated that the Confederate naval force at New Orleans consisted of the ram *Manassas,* one gunboat armed with six guns; four gunboats carrying two guns each; "one floating battery, made of a drydock cut down; carries 20 guns; three boats building, to be covered with railroad iron (said to be clumsy); six boats on Lake Pontchartrain and three others building." Farragut's picture of the Confederate ironclads was even hazier. "We have no definite knowledge of the ironclad steamers in New Orleans," he told Gideon Welles. "That they have partially clad the vessels there is no doubt, but we will endeavor to deal with them to the best advantage." Farragut had much better information on Forts Jackson and St. Philip, enabling him to cobble together a fairly accurate assessment of their strengths and weaknesses. [10]

As the time for the attack drew closer, Farragut had the men fasten chains on the sides of the ships to protect the machinery, whitewash the decks and gun carriages to make the guns and equipment easier to see at night, camouflage the hulls with oil and mud, and pack the spaces around the boilers and holds with bags of ashes and clothing and sand and whatever else they could think of.

When not drilling the men, exercising gun crews, laying in provisions, or studying the enemy's defenses, he was making the rounds. "Farragut was about the fleet from early dawn until dark," recalled John Russell Bartlett, then a midshipman doing lieutenant's duty on the *Brooklyn,* "and if any officers or men had not spontaneous enthusiasm he certainly infused it into them. I have been on the morning watch, from 4 to 8, when he would row alongside the ship at six o'clock, either hailing to ask how we were getting along, or, perhaps, climbing over the side to see for himself." Bartlett, who had never met Farragut before, was "much impressed with his energy and activity and his promptness of decision and action. He had a winning smile and a most charming manner and was jovial and talkative. . . . The officers who had the good fortune to be immediately associated with him seemed to worship him."[11]

Last but not least, Farragut got himself ready for battle. He expected to win. "As to being prepared for defeat," he wrote Virginia on April 11, "I certainly am not. Any man who is prepared for defeat would be half defeated before he commenced."[12] "I mean to be whipped or to whip my enemy," he noted later, "and not to be scared to death."[13] He accepted the possibility of death as the price of the endeavor. "I have now attained what I have been looking for all my life—a flag," he wrote Virginia, "and, having attained it, all that is necessary to complete the scene is a victory. If I die in the attempt, it will only be what every officer has to expect. He who dies in doing his duty to his country, and at peace with his God, has played out the drama of life to the best advantage."[14]

The fleet began moving up the Mississippi on April 14. By the sixteenth, all the ships had assembled at a point just below the Confederate defenses. On the seventeenth Farragut issued orders containing procedures for dealing with fire rafts and had numbers painted on the smokestacks of his ships so he could more easily distinguish them in battle.

Meanwhile, Coast Survey triangulation teams determined the optimum firing positions for the mortar schooners, and vessels were towed into place, concealed from the forts by a bend in the river and the thick forest ashore. The crews tied branches to the masts to camouflage the spotters observing the fire, reminding some of the men of Christmas decorations rather than preparation for battle.

Porter's mortars began a slow, steady bombardment of Forts Jackson and St. Philip on the evening of April 18. Some of Farragut's gunboats joined in. Confederate return fire hit a few vessels and wounded several men. Farragut's fleet signal officer,

Bradley Osbon, who had commanded a ship in the Argentine navy before the Civil War, discerned apprehension among the officers aboard one of the ships. Farragut ordered Osbon to pay them a visit. "Tell them some stories of the fights you've been in and come out of alive," he said. "It will stir their blood and do them good."[15]

On the morning of April 20, Farragut summoned all of his skippers to the flagship. When they all had arrived in the flag officer's cabin, Farragut laid out his plan of operations, using charts of the river and the forts. The squadron's seventeen sloops and gunboats, arrayed in three divisions, each in line-ahead formation, would steam past the forts through a breach in the obstructions, then engage and defeat whatever vessels the Confederates threw into the battle. With the squadron safely above the forts, the troops would land on the Gulf coast near Quarantine, march through the swamps to the river, rendezvous with the ships, and proceed upriver to New Orleans. Farragut intended to move out in the middle of the night so that the ships would be well past the forts by sunrise. The flagship *Hartford* would take the lead in the center division.

Nobody liked the idea of passing the forts without reducing them first. "Some of the captains thought it suicidal and believed that the whole fleet would be annihilated," recalled John Bartlett. Others thought that "perhaps one or two vessels might get by, but they would be sunk by the rams."[16] Still others worried that even if most of the ships got by, they might well run out of supplies before the forts fell and would then have to run the gauntlet of fire a second time.

Farragut disagreed. "Our ammunition is being rapidly consumed," he said. "Without a supply at hand, something must be done immediately. I believe in celerity." Despite the skippers' objections, Farragut intended to pass the forts, reduced or not, when, as he put it, "the propitious time has arrived."[17] That night, two of his gunboats opened a breach in the obstructions, cutting the chain with hammer and chisel.

After two days of bombardment, Forts Jackson and St. Philip

were still shooting back. The mortars hadn't silenced the enemy guns as Porter had claimed they would. The bombardment dragged on; three days passed, then four, still with no slackening of return fire from the forts, which killed two Union sailors and wounded thirty others.

Farragut grew impatient. On the morning of April 23, Porter came on board the *Hartford,* discouraged but still keen on continuing the bombardment. Farragut was skeptical. "Look here, David," he said. "We'll demonstrate the practical value of mortar work." He turned to his signal officer. "Mr. Osbon," he said, "get two small flags, a white one and a red one, and go to the mizzen topmasthead and watch where the mortar shells fall. If inside the fort, wave the red flag. If outside, wave the white one." Osbon complied. The "outs" won by a large majority. "There, David," Farragut said to Porter, "there's the score. I guess we'll go up the river to-night."[18] The propitious time had arrived.

That afternoon, Farragut visited each ship in the squadron to make sure the skippers understood his orders. He knew that in the thick of battle amid darkness and smoke, he wouldn't be able to communicate with them very well. He wanted every commander to understand exactly what he wanted them to do, so that each one could proceed independently if the need arose. His enthusiasm and determination inspired and encouraged the skippers, overcoming much of their apprehension.

Beneath Farragut's confident exterior, however, lurked fear for the men. That evening, he was standing on the quarterdeck, gazing upriver. After a spell he turned toward his signal officer. "What do you estimate our casualties will be, Mr. Osbon?" he asked.

"Flag-officer," said Osbon, "I have been thinking of that, and I believe we will lose a hundred."

The low figure surprised Farragut. "No more than that?" he said. "How do you calculate on so small a number?"

"Well," said Osbon, "most of us are pretty low in the water, and, being near, the enemy will shoot high. Then, too, we will be moving and it will be dark, with dense smoke. Another thing, gunners ashore are never as accurate as gunners aboard a vessel. I believe a hundred men will cover our loss."

Farragut stared at Osbon for a long moment before replying. "I wish I could think so," he said sadly. "I wish I could be as sure of it as you are."

Farragut turned and began pacing the deck. Osbon gazed up at the sky, wondering what the weather would bring that night, perhaps searching for words to comfort his commander. He spotted a bald eagle circling above the fleet. "Look there, Flag-officer!" he cried, "that is our national emblem. It is a sign of victory."[19] Farragut looked up, hoping it was true, praying that not too many of his men would have to die to make it so.

At five minutes before 2 A.M. on April 24, Osbon hoisted two red lanterns on the deck of the flagship, signaling the fleet to get under way. The *Pensacola,* the second ship in the van, seemed to be having trouble raising her anchors. Farragut grew impatient. "Damn that fellow!" he exclaimed. "I don't believe he wants to start."[20] Finally, at 3 A.M., the *Pensacola* began steaming upriver, followed by the rest of the squadron. The *Hartford* got under way at 3:25.

The gunboat *Cayuga,* the lead ship in the first division, passed through the obstructions at 3:30 as the moon came up. Ten minutes later, the forts and the ships opened fire. Porter's preliminary bombardment had burned all the woodwork in Fort Jackson and had torn things up generally, but had done little real damage beyond dismounting four guns and damaging eleven gun carriages. The stress of six days of bombardment, however, had exhausted the Confederate gunners. Their fatigue hampered their performance as Farragut's ships steamed by.

As the ships and forts blasted away at one another, the clouds of smoke belching forth at every discharge obscured targets and exacerbated the problem of navigating at night through a crooked river channel against a three-and-a-half-knot current. At some moments, blazing fire rafts, flashing guns, and bursting shells lit the scene like day. At others, the pall of smoke hanging over the water reduced visibility to ten feet. The Union formation quickly disintegrated into something more like a race than an orderly line. As they passed through the obstructions, some ships veered toward one bank or the other instead of following the ship ahead, others paused to fire into the forts, while still others poured on steam and sped pell-mell up the river. Some ships slipped past the forts with nary a scratch; others got hammered.

Fourteen of the seventeen ships made it past the forts. Of the three that didn't, two got fouled in the obstructions and one took a shot through her boiler. All three withdrew without being sunk.

As the *Hartford* took her turn, Farragut borrowed a pair of opera glasses from Bradley Osbon and climbed the mizzen rigging so he could see over the smoke. "With his feet on the ratlines and his back against the shrouds," Osbon recalled, "he stood there as cool and undisturbed as if leaning against a mantel in his own home."[21] Gunners in the forts poured it on as the *Hartford* passed by.

A shell struck the mainmast. "We can't afford to lose you, Flag Officer!" shouted Osbon. "They'll get you up there, sure." Farragut didn't budge. "Flag Officer," Osbon shouted, "they'll break my opera glasses, if you stay up there."

Farragut began to lean over to hand the glasses to Osbon.

"Oh, damn the glasses!" Osbon exclaimed. "It's you we want. Come down!"[22]

Farragut did so. Almost immediately a shell exploded in the spot where he had just been standing, cutting away some of the rigging. "Shot, shell, grape, and canister filled the air with deadly missiles," Osbon wrote. He recalled:

> It was like the breaking up of the universe, with the moon and all the stars bursting in our midst. As for seeing what the other vessels were doing, or what was going on about us, that was impossible. In that blinding smoke, and night, with everything flying in all directions, the only thing we could see was the flash of guns in our faces and the havoc on our own ship. Ropes were swinging, splinters were flying. . . At first the enemy's aim had been high, but now they lowered it until their fire began to cut us through.[23]

"It was impossible," Farragut recalled, "to see how each vessel was conducting itself."[24]

The *Hartford* had not yet passed Fort St. Philip when Farragut spotted a tug pushing a blazing fire raft toward the flagship. "Hard-a-port!" he shouted. The helmsman responded instantly, but the ship was too near shore, and her bow ran up hard on a mud bank.

With the *Hartford* now a sitting duck, the tug shoved the fire raft against her port side. The paint on the hull ignited, and the fire spread quickly up the rigging. Farragut clasped his hands and raised them above his head. "My God!" he shouted. "Is it to end in this way?"[25] Fortunately, the *Hartford* had grounded in a spot where the gunners ashore couldn't hit her.

Farragut got control of himself, then coolly walked up and down the deck, urging the men on as they fought the fire. Now and then flames would leap through the gunports and the men would jump back. "Don't flinch from that fire, boys!" Farragut shouted. "There's a hotter fire than that for those who don't do their duty!"[26]

Every man on the *Hartford* struggled to save the ship. The men assigned to the fire department fought the flames. The gunners blasted the tug out of the water. Bradley Osbon grabbed three shells and knelt down to unscrew their fuzes.

"Come, Mr. Osbon," exclaimed Farragut, "This is no time for prayer!"

"Flag Officer," Osbon replied, "if you'll wait a second you'll get the quickest answer to prayer ever you heard of."[27]

Osbon finished unscrewing the fuzes, then tossed the shells onto the fire raft. The shells exploded, blowing out the bottom and eliminating the source of the blaze. Crewmen with hoses, pumps, and buckets extinguished the fire on the flagship. Farragut's emphasis on damage control training had paid off. Meanwhile the *Hartford* backed off the mud bank and the men burst into cheers. The flagship continued upriver.

At about four o'clock, some of the Confederate ships joined the fray. The Confederate gunboat *McRae* traded broadsides with

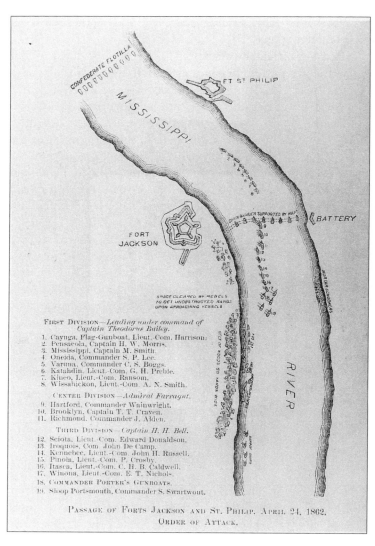

FIRST DIVISION—*Leading under command of*
Captain Theodorus Bailey.

1. Cayuga, Flag-Gunboat, Lieut.-Com. Harrison.
2. Pensacola, Captain H. W. Morris.
3. Mississippi, Captain M. Smith.
4. Oneida, Commander S. P. Lee.
5. Varuna, Commander C. S. Boggs.
6. Katahdin, Lieut.-Com. G. H. Preble.
7. Kineo, Lieut.-Com. Ransom.
8. Wissahickon, Lieut.-Com. A. N. Smith.

CENTER DIVISION—*Admiral Farragut.*

9. Hartford, Commander Wainwright.
10. Brooklyn, Captain T. T. Craven.
11. Richmond, Commander J. Alden.

THIRD DIVISION—*Captain H. H. Bell.*

12. Sciota, Lieut.-Com. Edward Donaldson.
13. Iroquois, Com. John De Camp.
14. Kennebec, Lieut.-Com. John H. Russell.
15. Pinola, Lieut.-Com. P. Crosby.
16. Itasca, Lieut.-Com. C. H. B. Caldwell.
17. Winona, Lieut.-Com. E. T. Nichols.
18. COMMANDER PORTER'S GUNBOATS.
19. Sloop Portsmouth, Commander S. Swartwout.

PASSAGE OF FORTS JACKSON AND ST. PHILIP, APRIL 24, 1862.
ORDER OF ATTACK.

Passage of Forts Jackson and St. Philip, April 24, 1862.
Naval Historical Center USN903009

two Union vessels until a shell exploded in her sail room and set her ablaze. Her skipper took her out of the fight while the crew put out the fire. The Confederate ironclad *Manassas* rammed two Union ships, missed a third, then turned back upriver when she reached the obstructions. Neither Union ship received serious damage, but Union fire riddled the ram's smokestack, greatly reducing her speed. Still, she managed to drive off four Union ships moving in to finish off the *McRae.* The *Louisiana,* anchored just above Fort St. Philip, traded shots with a few of the Union ships as they passed by.

Many of the Rebels' converted tugs and unarmed steamers turned tail and fled upstream at the sight of the advancing Union ships. The *Cayuga* soon caught up and got in among them, firing furiously. Three of the outgunned tugs caught fire, struck their colors, and ran ashore. The Union sloop *Oneida* and gunboat *Varuna* joined in the melee and sank several others.

The *Varuna* broke free of the pack and raced upriver. The Louisiana state gunboat *Governor Moore* took off in pursuit. At daybreak, the ships began firing on one another as the *Governor Moore* closed to ram. With the Yankee gunboat raking his ship with grape and shrapnel, the Rebel skipper order his bow gunners to depress their piece and fire through their own deck, and they then rammed the *Varuna.* After the *Governor Moore* rammed the *Varuna* a second time, the Rebel tug *Stonewall Jackson* rammed the *Varuna's* other side, inflicting fatal damage. Even as their ship went down, the *Varuna's* gunners kept pouring fire into their antagonists. They fatally damaged the *Stonewall Jackson,* whose skipper ordered her run ashore and burned. Meanwhile, other Union ships arrived on the scene and opened fire on the *Governor Moore,* whose skipper ran her ashore and had her set ablaze as well.

Union ships began arriving off Quarantine at 5:30. As the *Hartford* came up, Farragut, who had climbed back into the rigging, spotted the *Manassas* closing on his ships. Lieutenant George Dewey, future hero of Manila Bay, was standing with his skipper on the hurricane deck of the USS *Mississippi.* Dewey recalled that Farragut, "his face eager with victory in the morning light and his eyes snapping," shouted "Run down the ram!"[28] Realizing the hopelessness of the situation, the skipper of the *Manassas* ran his ship aground and ordered his men to escape.

The remaining Union ships arrived at Quarantine by 6 A.M. Loud cheers greeted each arrival. Farragut ordered the fleet to anchor and sent Marines ashore to take possession of the buildings. The men washed the sweat and powder grime from their hands and faces and ate breakfast. Then they washed the blood off the decks, buried their dead, and made some minor repairs.

The *Hartford* had taken eighteen hits and had two guns dismounted. Four other vessels had taken more than ten hits each. In all, Farragut's ships lost 37 men killed and 149 wounded while running the forts. The Confederates lost eight vessels, more than eighty men killed, and more than one hundred wounded. It was a resounding victory for Farragut.

Leaving two gunboats at Quarantine to wait for Butler's troops, Farragut got the remaining twelve ships under way at eleven o'clock. As the squadron steamed upriver, "the people on the banks [gazed] at us in blank astonishment," recalled Third Assistant Engineer Ralph Aston, serving on board the *Cayuga,* "some of them waving handkerchiefs at us and others looking spitefully at our waving flag. The darkeys in particular seemed overjoyed, dancing and clapping their hands and going through frantic gymnastical movements." As the gunboat passed one plantation, one of a group of ecstatic slaves pulled a U.S. flag out of his shirt and waved it over his head. "Three hearty and spontaneous cheers arose from the fleet at the sight," noted Aston, "enough to make the Rebels tremble if they heard it."[29] The ships anchored for the night at a point some twenty miles below New Orleans.

Upon receiving word that the ships had successfully passed the forts, the city's inhabitants set fire to thousands of bales of cotton and all manner of merchant vessels and small craft, to prevent them from falling into enemy hands. The streets filled with

USS *Hartford* in Mobile Bay, 1864, wearing the gray camouflage paint adopted by the Navy during the war.
Naval Historical Center

Battle of Mobile Bay by Julian Oliver Davidson, 1886. Chromolithograph. *The Lincoln Museum, Fort Wayne, Indiana*

USS *Hartford* and CSS *Tennessee. An August Morning with Farragut* by William Heysham Overend, 1883. Oil on canvas. *Naval Historical Center*

Farragut at the pinnacle of his career. Farragut and Captain Percival Drayton on board the *Hartford* after the battle of Mobile Bay, 1864. *Naval Historical Center*

Another view of Farragut and Drayton, leaning on the field carriage wheels of a Dahlgren boat gun. *Library of Congress*

AMERICAN NAVAL OFFICER GOING INTO ACTION—NEW STYLE
INVENTED BY COMMODORE FARRAGUT.

Caricature in *Frank Leslie's Illustrated Newspaper,* 10 September 1864.
U.S. Naval Academy Museum

Admiral David G. Farragut (seated, second from right) with former Union army leaders, at West End, New Jersey, 1868. General Philip Sheridan sits on Farragut's right. *Naval Historical Center*

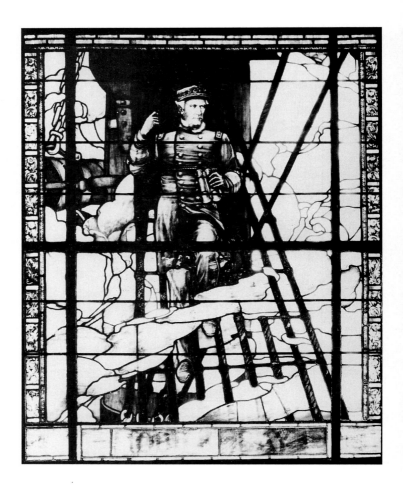

Portion of Admiral David G. Farragut Memorial Window, United States Naval Academy Chapel, by Frederick Wilson, 1914. Stained glass. *U.S. Naval Academy Museum*

crowds, some of whom looted barrels of rice, meat, sugar, and tobacco.

At about 5:30 on the morning of April 25, the ships raised anchor and got under way, steaming slowly upriver past hundreds of burning cotton bales and some twenty cotton-laden vessels drifting in the current. Upon rounding English Turn, just below the city, the squadron confronted the Chalmette fortifications, scene of Andrew Jackson's victory over the British in 1815 and now the city's last line of defense. The Confederate gunners fired a few rounds at the ships until a storm of broadsides drove them into the woods. The engagement lasted no more than twenty minutes.

As the squadron neared the city, rain clouds and smoke formed an arch over the river. Streams of fire from burning cotton and vessels along the banks carried up large amounts of debris that cascaded down on the decks as the ships steamed upriver with colors flying. It was a fitting end to one of the most triumphant voyages in American naval history.

The squadron rounded Slaughterhouse Point at about one o'clock. The mob on the levee cursed and screamed with rage. One of the men on shore recalled that no one on the ships said a word. "But one old tar on the *Hartford,* standing with lanyard in hand beside a great pivot-gun, so plain to view that you could see him smile," the man noted, "silently patted its big black breech and blandly grinned."[30] Burning steamers and barges continued to drift past the anchored fleet. Among the burning vessels was the unfinished Confederate ironclad *Mississippi.*

At three o'clock Farragut sent two officers ashore under a flag of truce to demand the city's surrender. As the officers approached City Hall, the mob nearly lynched them, but two prominent citizens intervened in the nick of time and saved their necks. The ranking Confederate officer announced that he would withdraw his troops, then the mayor could do what he pleased. At that, the two officers returned to the *Hartford.* Later that afternoon the band on the *Mississippi* struck up "The Star-

Spangled Banner." When some of the crowd began cheering and waving their hats, a troop of cavalry rode up and fired a volley into them. Farragut realized how tense the situation was and had every man in the fleet armed with a revolver and cutlass to stop any attempt at boarding that night.

After four days of negotiations, Farragut on the twenty-ninth sent an officer and all the marines in the fleet to City Hall to haul down the Louisiana state flag and raise the stars and stripes. That same morning, Farragut received word that Forts Jackson and St. Philip had surrendered and that the ironclad *Louisiana* had been blown up. Butler's troops had landed above Fort St. Philip on the twenty-seventh, precipitating a mutiny among the garrison of Fort Jackson that night. The forts had surrendered on the twenty-eighth.

General Butler arrived at New Orleans on May 1 and began to land his troops that afternoon. Mobs from the city jeered and hooted as the soldiers disembarked. The troops held them off with bayonets. Butler quartered his men in the center of town, on its principal squares, and on the levee.

Although Butler initially took a kid-glove approach to the occupation of New Orleans, very few city officials, bankers, merchants, or foreign consuls proved willing to cooperate with him in restoring normal life to the city. During the first few weeks of the occupation, a Union officer or enlisted man could scarcely board an omnibus or pass a lady on the sidewalk without encountering sneers of contempt.

One day Farragut and Fleet Surgeon Jonathan M. Foltz entered a crowded streetcar. Farragut sat down next to a well-dressed woman and her little daughter. Foltz remained standing nearby. The glittering gold braid on the flag officer's coat caught the little girl's eye. "Look, Mamma!" she exclaimed. "Pretty!"

Farragut, who was fond of children, laughingly patted her on the head. "You are a dear little girl," he said.

The girl's mother turned around, spat in Farragut's face, jerked the child away, and denounced him in language so filled with hate that Foltz feared she was going to attack the flag officer. The fleet surgeon grabbed her by the wrists and began to scold her for her conduct.

Farragut took Foltz by the arm. "Remember that this city is under the guns of my fleet," he said calmly, wiping his face with his handkerchief. "Many lives may be sacrificed and the city destroyed just because of this foolish woman, for she can easily provoke a riot. We must not think of ourselves but of the innocent who would suffer with the guilty."[31]

The woman blanched. Meanwhile, bystanders on the street who heard the angry voices ran up to the slowly moving streetcar and asked what was wrong. The woman said nothing. Farragut let the incident pass.

Such behavior led General Butler to doff the kid gloves and govern New Orleans with an iron fist. Two weeks after his arrival, he issued his infamous "Woman Order." "Hereafter when any female shall, by word, gesture, or movement, insult or show contempt for any officer or soldier of the United States," it declared, "she shall be regarded and held liable to be treated as a woman of the town plying her avocation."[32] The order brought the insults to Union officers and men to a screeching halt and earned Butler animosity throughout the South, where he was forever after known as the "Beast."

The fall of the Confederacy's largest city and most important port dealt Southern morale a severe blow. "New Orleans gone and with it the Confederacy!" wrote Mary Boykin Chesnut in her famous diary. "That Mississippi ruins us if it is lost!"[33]

The strategic consequences far outweighed the jolt to Southern morale and pride. The loss of New Orleans severely damaged Confederate diplomatic efforts to gain British and French recognition of Southern independence. It provided the Union with an excellent naval base for operations upriver and around the Gulf and cut a large chunk of the Confederacy off from access to the sea. "The bloodless surrender of New Orleans," as British military historian Liddell Hart put it, "was the thin end of a strategical wedge which split the Confederacy up the vital line of this great river."[34]

Confederate blunders contributed mightily to the city's fall. Richmond failed to appreciate the gravity of the situation confronting New Orleans when Farragut's ships began crossing the bar into the river. Stephen Mallory bears much of the blame, for his overestimation of the ability of forts to stop wooden ships, his shifting of troops and vessels upriver, and his failure to hasten completion of the ironclads *Mississippi* and *Louisiana* cost the defenders the potential means for staving off Farragut's attack. Blame also falls on the lack of unity of command among the various local Rebel naval and land forces, resulting in a poorly coordinated defense.

Certainly Gideon Welles and Gustavus Fox deserve much of the credit for conceiving and supporting the operation and for picking Farragut to lead it. And certainly Farragut's planning, logistical preparation, intelligence gathering, and emphasis on gunnery and damage control training made a successful outcome possible.

But more than anything else, it was Farragut's audacity in running the forts before they were reduced, when nearly everyone under his command doubted it could be done, that produced the most decisive naval victory of the Civil War.

Recognition came slowly to Farragut. The dust had barely settled around Forts Jackson and St. Philip when Porter and Butler began scrambling for the credit and sniping at one another. The newspapers heaped praise on "Porter's mortar boats" and "Butler's expedition" but ignored Farragut's squadron. For weeks only the Navy Department and Lincoln's Cabinet knew to whom the credit really belonged. Farragut mostly ignored Porter and Butler's bickering. He was too busy planning his next move.

Chapter 5

Purgatory on the Mississippi

FARRAGUT'S INITIAL INSTRUCTIONS directed him to "push a strong force up the river to take all their defenses in the rear" as well as to "reduce the fortifications which defend Mobile Bay."[1] Farragut figured he would send the lighter-draft gunboats and the sloop *Brooklyn* up the Mississippi and use the rest of his heavier vessels along with Porter's mortar flotilla against Mobile. On May 2, he began dispatching gunboats upriver, with a view toward capturing Vicksburg.

Five days later Farragut embarked on the *Hartford* and headed upriver himself. The squadron raised the stars and stripes at Baton Rouge on the ninth and at Natchez on the thirteenth. General Butler dispatched some 1,400 troops under Brigadier General Thomas Williams to occupy points reduced by the fleet. On May 20 Farragut boarded the gunboat *Kennebec* and stood upriver for a look at Vicksburg's defenses.

Above and below Vicksburg the Mississippi River looped crazily through the countryside. A rather straight line of bluffs running along western Mississippi touched the river at Vicksburg and Grand Gulf. Vicksburg itself lay atop bluffs that rose two hundred feet above the east bank of the river, overlooking a horse-shoe bend upstream and a 6-mile-long straight run downstream.

Farragut learned that the Confederates had mounted ten guns below Vicksburg and two above, with two gunboats lying under the latter. On May 23 he ordered five of his own gunboats to go up and cut out or destroy the Confederate vessels. Three of his skippers demurred, arguing that it was "impractical" or "madness" to attempt such a thing.[2]

Farragut boarded the *Kennebec* for another look at the defenses on the twenty-fourth. This time he saw fourteen guns arrayed in three batteries. The next day Farragut conferred with his skippers and General Williams. Everyone realized that the ships' guns couldn't be elevated enough to reach the batteries on the highest bluffs. Williams said that his own force was inadequate to overcome the eight thousand Confederate soldiers he believed were in Vicksburg. Farragut decided not to attack. He left six gunboats below the city to blockade the river. The rest of the squadron along with the Army transports headed back downriver. The troops landed at Baton Rouge. The *Hartford* continued down to New Orleans, arriving there on May 30.

In New Orleans Farragut encountered a pile of mail from the Navy Department, both congratulating him for capturing the Crescent City and berating him for not yet pressing upriver to Memphis to meet the Western Flotilla, the name of the Union gunboat force now under Foote's successor, Flag Officer Charles H. Davis. "The President of the United States requires you to use your utmost exertions (without a moment's delay, and before any other naval operations shall be permitted to interfere)," said a directive from Secretary Welles dated May 19, "to open the river Mississippi and effect a junction with Flag-Officer Davis."[3]

These orders took Farragut aback. Although he had known from the beginning that he would have to push up the Mississippi, he had never thought he would have to go farther than Natchez. Evidently, Washington was oblivious to the difficulties inherent in operating big oceangoing ships in the river.

Farragut wasn't particularly worried about Confederate batteries, for he didn't expect to encounter anything more formidable than the forts below New Orleans. The chief problem lay in maintaining his line of communications "over a long, narrow, tortuous, and very difficult road, passing in many places close under the guns of the enemy," as naval historian and officer Alfred Thayer Mahan put it.

> To take the defenses in the rear and . . . drive the enemy out of them, was one thing; but to hold the abandoned positions against the return of the defenders, after the fleet had passed on, required an adequate force which Butler's army. . . could not afford. Coal and supply ships, therefore, must either run the gauntlet for the four hundred miles which separated Vicksburg from New Orleans, or be accompanied always by armed vessels. The former alternative was incompatible with the necessary security, and for the latter the numbers of the fleet were utterly inadequate. In fact, to maintain the proposed operations, there would be needed so many more ships to guard the communications that there would be none left for the operations to which they led.[4]

Farragut intended to go to Memphis as ordered, but he wasn't happy about it. On June 3, he sent Welles dispatches describing in detail the pitfalls of operating in the river. He outlined problems arising from lack of pilots; procuring and distributing coal; guerrilla activities along the banks; falling water threatening to trap his heavy ships till next spring; clamoring of sailors whose enlistments were up to go home; breakdowns of machinery; ships grounding; ships colliding; ships in need of repair; ships losing anchors; everything. "The danger and difficulties of the river," he declared, "have proved to us since we first entered it much greater impediments to our progress and more destructive to our vessels than the enemy's shot."[5]

Farragut abandoned any ideas for operations against Mobile until the Mississippi lay in Union hands. From reports of enemy activity by his skippers and from deserters, he concluded that the Confederates intended to make "the final stand" for "the defense of this river" at Vicksburg.[6] He made preparations to return there with a stronger combined force. He ordered Porter to bring ten mortar schooners to Vicksburg to bombard the batteries on the bluffs. Butler beefed up General Williams's command to three thousand soldiers.

On June 8 Farragut started upriver on board the *Hartford.* Within a week he received the welcome news that Memphis had fallen to Flag Officer Davis and the not so welcome news that the Confederate ram *Arkansas,* under construction on the Yazoo River, mounted twenty guns and was nearly ready for service.

At 7:45 on the morning of June 25, the *Hartford* dropped anchor seven miles below Vicksburg. Three of Farragut's sloops and nine of his gunboats had already arrived, as had seventeen mortar schooners and six steamers under Porter. Later that morning the troopships appeared.

The Confederates, meanwhile, had strengthened Vicksburg's defenses, which now included twenty-nine guns arrayed in six batteries. Two of the batteries stood above the town on the outer bank of the horseshoe bend, with the guns sited to rake vessels approaching from either upstream or downstream. The other four batteries stood below the town, with the guns sited to pour plunging fire on vessels in the river below. Thus, ships attempting to pass the batteries from downriver would face fire from ahead and from starboard. Some ten thousand Confederate soldiers stood by in near-supporting distance of the batteries in expectation of a land attack on Vicksburg.

Farragut issued his plan of operations shortly after arriving on the twenty-fifth. After a preliminary bombardment by Porter's mortars, the squadron would run past the batteries as at New Orleans. Once above the city, the squadron could proceed to Memphis as ordered. Farragut intended to array his ships in two parallel lines, with the sloops *Richmond, Hartford,* and *Brooklyn* to the right and one sloop and seven gunboats to the left. The lines would be staggered so that the ships to port could fire on the enemy batteries without hitting the ships to starboard.

The mortar schooners opened fire on June 26 and kept up a slow bombardment for two days. This time Porter made no predictions about when or even if they would silence the batteries ashore.

At 2 A.M. on the twenty-eighth, Farragut ordered two red lights hoisted at the mizzen, the same signal to get under way as at New Orleans. Two hours later the mortars fired as rapidly as possible while the lead ships began to engage the enemy. As at Forts Jackson and St. Philip, smoke quickly enveloped the ships, compounding the problems of navigating and shooting in the darkness. Gunners tried to fire at muzzle flashes, but in the confusion they were just as likely to fire at the flashes made by exploding shells. Fire from passing ships only temporarily silenced the batteries ashore. The Confederates suffered only thirteen casualties, and none of their guns were disabled.

The *Hartford* entered the fray at about 4:15, with Farragut again standing in his favorite spot in the mizzen rigging. Confederate projectiles cut the captain's cabin to pieces, killed one man and wounded eleven others, and nearly got Farragut. A gun captain behind Farragut on the poop deck wished to fire in his direction, so he hailed the flag officer and asked him to descend. Farragut climbed down. He had barely reached the deck when a shell cut away all the mizzen rigging where he had just been standing. He got away with a blow on the head that did not break the skin. The *Hartford,* too, escaped serious injury.

At about twenty past six the flagship came to anchor some three or four miles above Vicksburg. All but four of Farragut's ships were present. One gunboat had gone ahead to the mouth of the Yazoo; the *Brooklyn* and two gunboats had not made it past the batteries. When Farragut later upbraided the *Brooklyn's* skipper, Captain Thomas T. Craven, Craven requested to be relieved of command. Farragut did so. "Some are bitter against me," he wrote of skippers like Craven, "because I tell them when I think they don't do their duty. . . . My fault is not oppression, but being too lenient; but a man *must* do his work, particularly when that work is *fighting,* and if he doesn't I'll tell him of it. I don't want such men under my command, and am too glad for them to go

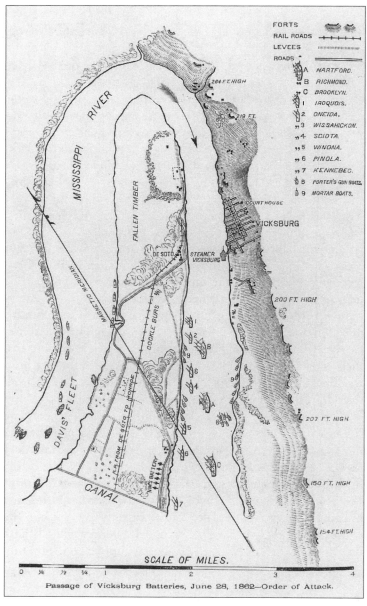

Passage of Vicksburg batteries, June 28, 1862.
Naval Historical Center NH59031

home and get their 'rights.'" [7] Union naval forces lost a total of
sixteen men killed and forty-six wounded during the battle. The
uninjured "spliced the main brace."

Later that morning Farragut sent a brief report to Welles,
reflecting his frustration with Washington's "peremptory" orders
to "free the river of all impediments," as he put it to Davis. "I
passed up the river this morning," he wrote Welles, "but to no
purpose. The enemy leave their guns for the moment, but return
to them as soon as we have passed and rake us. . . . I am satisfied
that it is not possible for us to take Vicksburg without an army
force of twelve or fifteen thousand men. General Van Dorn's division is here and lies safely behind the hills. The water is too low
for me to go over 12 or 15 miles above Vicksburg." [8] That same
morning Farragut also wrote to Major General Henry W. Halleck, commander of Army forces in the Western Theater, request-
ing assistance. Farragut assumed Halleck would send help and
intended to renew the attack once the troops arrived.

Three days later (July 1), as Farragut was eating breakfast,
lookouts sighted leading elements of the Western Flotilla heading
downstream. It was the first time Farragut had seen the city-class
ironclads *Benton, Carondelet, Cincinnati,* and *Louisville.* "The
iron-clads are curious things to us salt-water gentlemen," he
wrote. "They look like great turtles." [9] Fifteen minutes later four
river steamers, three tugs, four mortar boats, and two hospital
boats came into view. Sailors from both fleets cheered at the sight
of each other. The meeting of the fleets meant that Farragut had
carried out his orders to the letter.

The next afternoon Davis's mortar vessels opened fire on
Vicksburg. On July 3 both Davis's and Porter's mortars fired
intermittently on the city all day. At midnight, each vessel in both
fleets ushered in Independence Day with a national salute of
thirty-four guns.

Later that day, Davis invited Farragut to join him in his flagship, the *Benton,* for a go at the Confederate batteries. Farragut
accepted. When the ironclad reached a good position, she opened
fire. Confederate batteries ashore returned fire and soon put a

shell through one of the *Benton*'s bow ports. The shell exploded, killing or wounding several men. "Damn it, Davis, I must go on deck!" Farragut shouted. "I feel as though I were shut up here in an old iron pot, and I can't stand it!"[10] He did so. Soon, Davis persuaded him to take shelter in the pilot house.

The next several days passed with nothing more exciting than a few desultory exchanges with the Confederate batteries. General Halleck's reply arrived at this time. "The scattered and weakened condition of my forces," he wrote, "renders it impossible for me at the present to detach any troops to cooperate with you on Vicksburg."[11] So much for help from the Army, without which the city couldn't be taken.

Meanwhile, the summer heat was lengthening the sick lists daily as dysentery, dengue, and malaria ravaged the fleet. Farragut, too, fell ill. Reports that the Confederates had fortified the bluffs at Grand Gulf, Fort Adams, and Ellis Cliffs meant that gunboats now had to accompany all the transports bringing supplies upriver. The water in the Mississippi had already fallen sixteen feet. If it dropped much lower, Farragut would be unable to get his heavy ships out of the river till next spring.

Farragut decided to get out while the getting was good. On July 10, he wrote Welles asking for permission to withdraw. With no Confederate naval vessels left to threaten communications save the *Arkansas,* and with Davis's flotilla perfectly adequate for maintaining communications and blockading Vicksburg, there was no reason to stay. Once back in the Gulf, Farragut could prosecute the blockade more effectively and commence operations against Mobile.

Welles was of the same mind. On July 14, he instructed Farragut to withdraw from the Mississippi, proceed to the Gulf, and operate "at such point or points on the Southern coast as you may deem advisable."[12] These orders crossed Farragut's request in the mail.

Farragut doubted that the *Arkansas* would ever emerge from the Yazoo. Even so, he figured he ought to dispatch an expedition to investigate a claim from two Confederate deserters that the ironclad was scheduled to steam down the Yazoo on July 15. On the same day that Welles wrote the order to withdraw, Farragut held a conference on board the *Hartford* with Flag Officer Davis, General Williams, and Colonel Alfred W. Ellet, who commanded a fleet of small rams attached to Davis's flotilla. They decided to send the ironclad gunboat *Carondelet,* the wooden gunboat Tyler, and the Ellet ram *Queen of the West* up the Yazoo the next morning.

The deserters were right. The Confederates had just finished preparing the *Arkansas* for battle. The ironclad measured 165 feet long by 35 feet wide, drew eleven and a half feet of water, mounted ten guns, and wore four and a half inches of railroad iron. She was long, low, and rakish. On the very day Farragut was planning the expedition up the Yazoo, the Rebels were finalizing plans to send the *Arkansas* down the Yazoo, through the Yankee flotillas, and on to Vicksburg.

At four in the morning of July 15, the *Carondelet, Tyler,* and *Queen of the West* got under way. They reached the mouth of the Yazoo at 5:45 and stood upriver. At 7:00 A.M. they encountered the *Arkansas* bearing down on them. The overmatched Yankee ships came about, trading shots with the Rebel ram as they fled. The *Carondelet* was driven ashore. The *Tyler* and *Queen of the West* managed to stay about two hundred yards ahead of the *Arkansas,* which soon entered the Mississippi.

Farragut heard the gunfire, but figured it was an engagement between the gunboats and Confederate mobile artillery said to be operating on the banks above Vicksburg. Davis reached the same conclusion. None of their ships got up steam, loaded their guns, nor made any other preparations for battle.

Suddenly at 8:30 lookouts spotted the *Tyler* and *Queen of the West* rounding the point. Smoke poured from their funnels as they ran for their lives, with the *Arkansas* in hot pursuit. The other Union ships immediately beat to quarters and loaded their guns, but could not get up steam before the *Arkansas* passed them. The Rebel ram traded shots with the Yankee ships as she steamed by. The sound of the flagship's guns brought a surprised Farragut up to the deck in his nightshirt. Yankee gunfire perforated the *Arkansas's* smokestack, shattered her pilot house, and twice penetrated her armor, but did not stop her. The battered ironclad soon reached the safety of Vicksburg's batteries.

Embarrassed at being caught with his pants down, Farragut wanted to take his whole fleet out immediately to destroy the Rebel ram. Davis persuaded him to wait until late in the afternoon, to make better preparations.

At seven that evening, Farragut's entire fleet got under way and headed downstream, arrayed in two columns, with the ships in the same order and in the same formation as they had been when they had come upriver. "No one will do wrong who lays his vessel alongside of the enemy or tackles with the ram," wrote Farragut in his general order to the fleet. "The ram must be destroyed."[13] But darkness had settled by the time the fleet reached the upper battery, and no one could find the *Arkansas,* even though the port column passed within thirty yards of the shore. A few broadsides from the ships silenced the Confederate batteries as they passed, but not before Rebel gunners disabled one gunboat and put a couple of shots into another, killing five men and wounding sixteen. Davis's flotilla, which played a supporting role, lost thirteen killed, thirty-four wounded, and ten missing.

The crew of the *Brooklyn* cheered as the ships arrived below Vicksburg, but Farragut's spirits remained low. Mortified at being surprised, he regretted that he hadn't gone after the ironclad straight away as he had wanted. "I will continue to . . . try to destroy her," he vowed in a dispatch to Davis the next day, "until my squadron is destroyed or she is." Later that day he proposed to Davis that they both launch an attack on the ram, "regardless of consequences to ourselves."[14]

Davis preferred a more cautious course. "The *Arkansas* is harmless in her present position," he replied, "and will be more easily destroyed should she come out from under the batteries than while enjoying their protection." Over the next few days Farragut kept trying to goad Davis into action. "I feel there is no rest for the wicked until she is destroyed," he wrote. But Davis remained opposed to any scheme for attacking the ram while she remained under Vicksburg's guns. "I think patience as great a virtue as boldness," he replied.[15]

To his wife, Davis wrote that Farragut's urging to attack the *Arkansas* "regardless of the consequences" came from a man who does not "rule over his own spirit." "Yet you must not think that Farragut and I differ unkindly," Davis added. "Nothing can exceed his kindness, candor, and liberality; our old ties have been strengthened by our present intercourse. He is a man who unites with a bold and impetuous spirit an affectionate temper, and a generous and candid nature."[16]

The waiting nearly drove Farragut mad. At last he could stand it no more. On the morning of July 21, the hottest day of the summer, he went to see Davis in person. They talked for hours. Farragut finally persuaded him to launch an attack the next day.

The ships got under way at three in the morning of the twenty-second. At daylight, three of Davis's ironclads moved in to shell the upper batteries while a fourth ironclad, the *Essex*, and the *Queen of the West* attempted to destroy the *Arkansas*. Farragut's fleet was to pounce after the *Essex* and *Queen of the West* had driven their prey downriver. Instead the *Essex* and *Queen of the West* got shot up by the shore batteries, but not before blasting a large hole in the *Arkansas*'s armor. Nevertheless, the Rebel ironclad lived to fight another day. Farragut's fleet managed only a few rounds into the Rebel batteries before the *Essex* appeared. It was another dismal failure.

The next day Farragut received welcome news from Washington, a telegram from Welles. "Go down river at discretion," it said. "Not expected to remain up during the season."[17]

"At last the Department appears to have waked up to the fact that we have no business up this river," Farragut wrote his wife. "I am most thankful," he added, "although it is most mortifying to leave the ram behind me undestroyed."[18]

Farragut wasted no time in departing. Early in the morning of July 25, his ships proceeded downriver, arrayed in two columns, with General Williams's men embarked on transports. The voyage passed uneventfully. After leaving Williams and his men at Baton Rouge, Farragut arrived at New Orleans at noon on the twenty-eighth. Three days later, Davis took his own flotilla up to the mouth of the Yazoo. Despite his having sanctioned the retreat, Welles considered the *Arkansas*'s descent and both squadrons' abandonment of Vicksburg "the most disreputable naval affair of the War."[19]

Farragut hoped shortly to get the bulk of his fleet out into the Gulf, where the salt air would revive his sick sailors, but Confederate operations kept him in the Mississippi. On August 1 he received a dispatch that the *Arkansas* and six thousand Rebel soldiers were advancing on Baton Rouge. At two in the morning of August 3, the *Arkansas* cast off. Forty-eight hours later, Rebel soldiers attacked Baton Rouge, killing or wounding some 250 of General Williams's 2,500 effective troops and putting a minie ball through Williams's heart. Only gunfire from the *Essex* averted disaster. Engine trouble kept the *Arkansas* from making an appearance.

News of the attack reached Farragut at midnight. Five and a half hours later, he departed New Orleans on board the *Hartford* and headed upriver, followed by several other vessels. News that the *Arkansas* had been destroyed greeted him upon his arrival at Baton Rouge at noon on the seventh. After the *Essex* had broken up the Rebel attack on the city, she steamed upriver to deal with the *Arkansas*. In maneuvering to meet her, the Rebel ironclad broke a connecting rod and drifted ashore, able to bring only one gun to bear. Her crew fired the gun, then fired the ship and set her adrift. The explosion of the Confederate ironclad's magazine ended the most embarrassing episode of Farragut's Civil War service.

At sunrise on August 9 the *Hartford* and two other ships headed downstream. Rebels in Donaldsonville, Louisiana, had repeatedly fired on transports in spite of warnings that if they continued to do so, the squadron would destroy the town. Upon arriving, the Union ships fired a few rounds into the town, then sent an expedition ashore to torch the hotels, wharves, and a guer-

Lieutenant David Glasgow Farragut, USN. Engraving after an oil portrait by William Swain, 1838. *U.S. Naval Academy Museum*

Loyall and Virginia Farragut, c. 1850. U.S. *Naval Academy Museum*

Rear Admiral David Glasgow Farragut, USN, 1862. *National Archives*

The Battle of New Orleans, 24 April 1862. *Farragut's Fleet* by Mauritz Frederik de Haas, n.d. Oil on canvas. *The Historic New Orleans Collection*

CSS *Arkansas* running through two Union fleets above Vicksburg, 15 July 1862. Line engraving after a drawing by Julian Oliver Davidson, c. 1887. *Naval Historical Center*

Rear Admiral David Glasgow Farragut, USN, 1862.
U.S. Naval Academy Museum

Bombardment of Port Hudson from the Confederate perspective, 14–15 March 1863. USS *Mississippi* burns at rear of Federal line. Engraving from *Harper's Weekly*, 1863. *Naval Historical Center*

Carte de visite, c. 1864, presented by Farragut to John H. Brooks, his African American steward. *U.S. Naval Academy Museum*

rilla leader's house. Retaliation of this sort was the only defense against flying batteries, sharpshooters, and guerrillas whose occasional potshots took a steady toll of Yankee sailors. Rebel leaders protested return fire because it endangered innocent women and children. "You chose your own time and place for the attack upon our defenseless people," Farragut replied to one such protester, "and should, therefore, see that the innocent and defenseless of your own people are out of the way before you make the attack, for rest assured that the fire will be returned and we will not hold ourselves answerable for the death of the innocent." [20] After burning Donaldsonville, Farragut continued on to New Orleans.

On August 12, news arrived that Farragut had been promoted to rear admiral, a rank created by Congress the previous July 16 to bring the Navy's rank structure in line with that of the Army. Farragut was ecstatic. "I hoisted my flag on the main," he wrote Virginia, "and the whole fleet cheered." [21] The promotion made Farragut the first rear admiral in American naval history. The next day the *Hartford* got under way and headed for the Gulf.

On August 20, the *Hartford* dropped anchor at Pensacola. Almost immediately Farragut began preparations to take Mobile. But new instructions from Secretary Welles dashed all hope of doing so in the near future. With a small Union force in New Orleans and a large Confederate army in northern Mississippi, Welles considered affairs in the lower Mississippi River "unsettled." His instructions emphasized the importance of supporting the Army in holding New Orleans and retaining control of the lower Mississippi. "These are objects of more importance than any other which may be at present in view in that quarter," he wrote. [22] The instructions also emphasized the importance of maintaining the blockade.

Farragut remained in Pensacola for three months. Although he was disappointed at having to postpone operations against Mobile, the Gulf breezes, delightful weather, and respite from combat reinvigorated him and restored his health. Before this time Farragut had neglected the blockade, largely because the

Navy Department had made it clear that opening the Mississippi took precedence. Welles understood the difficulty Farragut faced in simultaneously blockading the Gulf and keeping the Mississippi open with his limited force and promised to send him more ships as they became available.

Blockading the Confederate coast and combined operations with the Union army constituted the Union navy's principal missions during the Civil War. For most of the war, the blockade resembled a sieve that caught only the slowest or unluckiest ships. Five out of six blockade runners got through. Those that made it constituted the lifeline of the Confederacy. They supplied the Rebels with more than 60 percent of their small arms, one-third of the lead they used for bullets, and over two-thirds of their supply of saltpeter, an essential element of gunpowder.

Yet the blockade seriously undermined the Confederate economy. It reduced the South's seaborne trade to less than a third of its prewar level at a time when demand for goods far exceeded the peacetime norm. It also contributed to the ruinous inflation that so eroded the Confederate dollar that, by March 1863, it took ten dollars to buy what one had bought two years earlier.

"I confess blockading is a most disagreeable business," Farragut wrote, "but, if we had nothing but agreeable things to do in war, everybody would be in the Navy, and no one would be worthy of reward or promotion." [23] Union steamers easily picked off sailing ships. But the technological evolution of steam-powered blockade runners outpaced the tactical evolution of the blockade. Improvements in engineering, hull design, and camouflage gave blockade runners an edge in speed, maneuverability, and stealth over their pursuers.

Fortunately for Farragut, the volume of blockade running in the Gulf never equaled that of the Atlantic coast. After New Orleans fell, the shallow bars and channels in the remaining Gulf ports limited the draft of blockade runners to no more than twelve feet. Limited draft meant smaller vessels and less profitability. Moreover, English shippers preferred using the British colonies of Bermuda and Nassau rather than Spanish-controlled

Havana for transshipping cargoes from big, transatlantic vessels into smaller, fleeter blockade runners. And Confederate government policy favored East Coast ports.

Nevertheless, Farragut had his work cut out for him. In 1862, 65 percent of the vessels that attempted to run the blockade of the Gulf ports succeeded. When Farragut entered the Mississippi, he left behind only five steamers and a dozen or so sailing ships to patrol the coast from Pensacola to the Rio Grande. When he emerged from the river in August, all but two or three of his vessels needed a month or two of repairs. Bad weather, bad food, disease, and dull duty gnawed away continuously at his men and ships. Farragut himself strongly disliked doing the kind of administrative work necessary to keep the squadron supplied.

Yet he made a success of it. With New Orleans under Union control, Mobile and Galveston became the Confederacy's principal ports in the region. By November 1, 1862, Farragut's ships had captured some fifty-four blockade runners, mostly outward-bound sailing vessels loaded with cotton heading for Havana. By the end of 1862, Farragut had some two dozen steamers on blockade duty, with roughly half stationed off Mobile and Galveston and the rest scattered throughout the Gulf.

Blockade runners used every trick in the book, from flying false colors to giving false testimony. Farragut heard 'em all. On October 28, the USS *Montgomery* sighted a vessel flying English colors off Mobile. When the vessel refused to stop, the *Montgomery* gave chase. Although the runner's crew tossed cargo overboard to lighten ship, the blockader slowly gained on her. Some six hours into the chase, the *Montgomery* got within range and opened fire. After taking two hits, the prey hove to. She proved to be the *Caroline,* a former American steamer now under provisional English registry. The *Montgomery* took her into Pensacola and sent her skipper on board the *Hartford.*

It turned out that Farragut knew the skipper, one of the most experienced merchant captains in the Gulf. Farragut listened with obvious amusement as the fellow swore up one side and down the other that he was really bound for Matamoros, in Mexico.

"What in the world are you doing so close in to Mobile, three hundred miles out of your course," asked Farragut, "when your proposed destination was Matamoros?" The skipper gave a long-winded account of how he had been "swept in-shore by a north-east gale."

Farragut smiled good-naturedly and put his hand on the man's shoulder. "How could you be blown to the northward and eastward by a northeast gale?" he asked. "I am sorry for you, but we shall have to hold you for your damned bad navigation. Any man bound for Matamoros from Havana and coming within twelve miles of Mobile light has no business to have a steamer." [24] Farragut dispatched the *Caroline* to Philadelphia, where a prize court condemned her as a blockade runner.

Farragut preferred to blockade ports from inside a harbor, bar, or inlet. After two of his ships captured Sabine Pass on September 24, 1862, five gunboats under Commander William B. Renshaw applied this tactic at Galveston, closing the port by maintaining a presence at the harbor's entrance. The tactic worked until Confederate forces drove off Renshaw's flotilla on New Year's Eve. Renshaw lost two ships and his life in the bargain.

On January 11, 1863, the USS *Hatteras* spotted a suspicious-looking vessel off Galveston and gave chase. When the *Hatteras* had drawn well away from the other blockaders, the mysterious vessel came about and opened fire. The stranger proved to be the CSS *Alabama,* the most famous—or, from the Union perspective, infamous—commerce raider of all time, skippered by the flinty, petulant, mustache-twisting Raphael Semmes, the Confederate navy's most colorful character. The *Alabama* sank the *Hatteras* after a brief engagement, then vanished into the vast ocean to continue her odyssey of destruction.

Five days later another Confederate naval exploit embarrassed Farragut. The previous September, the CSS *Florida,* perhaps the second most famous (or infamous) Rebel raider, had slipped past the blockade into Mobile in broad daylight. On January 16, 1863, she slipped back out to begin her own odyssey of destruction.

Loyall Farragut, now nearly nineteen, had joined the West Gulf Blockading Squadron the previous fall to serve as his father's clerk on board the *Hartford*. "Pa has been very much worried at these things," Loyall wrote his mother about the disasters in the Gulf, "but still he bears it like a philosopher."[25]

David Farragut, meanwhile, returned to New Orleans, arriving there on November 9, 1862. Although the interval in Pensacola had enabled him to rest and get badly needed repairs done to his ships, he had tired of blockade duty. Initially, Farragut tried to persuade Ben Butler to participate in a combined expedition against Mobile, but Butler was relieved a month later amid rumors of corruption and controversies with foreign consuls.

Butler's successor, Major General Nathaniel P. Banks, arrived in New Orleans on December 15 with vague and conflicting orders to open the Mississippi and attack Mobile. Banks brought with him a letter from Abraham Lincoln to Farragut, ordering the admiral to assist him. Farragut took it to mean that he was to support the Army in attacking Vicksburg and Port Hudson.

The Confederates had been developing Port Hudson into another Mississippi stronghold, a Vicksburg in miniature. Port Hudson lay about a dozen miles above Baton Rouge on the east bank, facing an abrupt 90-degree bend in the river. Nineteen heavy guns and thirty-five field pieces situated on bluffs eighty to one hundred feet high lined the east bank for a mile and a half below the city. Some six thousand soldiers garrisoned the town. These defenses, together with Vicksburg's, enabled the Confederates to control the long stretch of the Mississippi in between, including the junction with the Red River, and to feed their armies with supplies from the southwest and Mexico.

Although Banks was just as gentlemanly as Butler was boorish, he proved no more willing than the Beast to mount risky operations. Farragut spent the winter of 1862–1863 preparing his fleet at New Orleans for an expedition to Port Hudson and waiting for Banks to move.

And waiting and waiting. Unbeknownst to Farragut, Banks

had decided not to attack Port Hudson because a deserter had convinced him that the garrison numbered more than thirty thousand.

The ships in the upper Mississippi, however, had not remained idle. The Western Flotilla had been under Army control since its creation. Welles and Fox had been lobbying to have it transferred to the Navy ever since, and this finally happened in October 1862. In a long-planned move, Charles Davis returned to Washington to become chief of the Bureau of Navigation. To relieve him in command of the flotilla, renamed the Mississippi Squadron, the Navy Department chose David D. Porter.

In December Porter commenced a series of long and arduous but ultimately brilliant operations to capture Vicksburg in conjunction with Major General Ulysses S. Grant, who in the fall of 1862 had succeeded Halleck in command of Army forces in the Western Theater. In February 1863, Porter ran the *Queen of the West* and the ironclad gunboat *Indianola* past Vicksburg to secure the Mississippi between there and Port Hudson, but the Confederates soon captured both ships, thereby strengthening their own control over that part of the Mississippi.

News of the disaster spurred Farragut into action. "The time has come!" he exclaimed. "There must be no more delay! I must go, army or no army."[26] He intended to steam to Port Hudson, run past the Confederate batteries there, recapture the ships Porter had lost, and cut off the flow of Confederate supplies down the Red River and across the Mississippi, particularly Texas beef.

Farragut had objected to operating on the Mississippi in 1862 because he felt the Army hadn't committed enough troops and the Navy couldn't accomplish anything significant without them. But with Grant and Porter fully engaged in the campaign against Vicksburg, Farragut considered it a strategic necessity, though still a tactical evil, to operate on the Mississippi in support of their efforts in 1863.

Early in March, Farragut led three sloops, five gunboats, an ironclad, six mortar schooners, and a dozen or so transports upriver. The flotilla arrived off Baton Rouge on the morning of the thirteenth. For the rest of the day, Farragut visited each ship to ensure that all was ready for battle.

At ten o'clock in the morning of March 14, Farragut gathered his skippers on board the flagship to ensure that each one understood his order for passing the batteries. "I think the best protection against the enemy's fire," it said, "is a well-directed fire from our own guns."[27]

Acting Volunteer Lieutenant John C. Parker, one of the junior officers present that day, thought that Farragut "presented a perfect picture of an ideal sailor." The admiral's "figure was faultless," the junior officer recalled many years later, "and dressed with the neatness and care customary in the Navy, he appeared much younger than he was." His face "lighted with a smile when returning the salute of the officers," making "an indelible impression, a mental photograph which time has never affected."[28]

Farragut intended to try a new tactical arrangement, lashing his weaker vessels to the port side of the bigger ships. Not only would this shelter the smaller ships from the storm of fire from the east bank as they steamed upstream, but it also gave each pair a chance to maneuver out of danger if one of the ship's engines took a fatal hit. The mortar vessels were to shell Port Hudson while the fleet ran past the Rebel batteries. Farragut convinced the reluctant Banks to cooperate by making a reconnaissance in force.

Early that evening, Fleet Surgeon Foltz asked Farragut to permit Loyall to assist him below with the wounded during the battle in the most protected part of the ship. "No, that will not do," replied Farragut. "He will act as one of my aids, to assist in conveying my orders during the battle, and we will trust in Providence and *la fortune de la guerre.*"[29]

At about nine o'clock, Farragut sent Loyall below to inform the fleet captain, Captain Thornton A. Jenkins, that he was ready to get under way. Jenkins had just finished a letter home, and Loyall found him absorbed in thought. Loyall returned to the quarterdeck. "Captain Jenkins looked very serious when I called him," he said to his father.

Farragut placed his hand on Loyall's shoulder. "Well, my son," he said, "Captain Jenkins has a family, and is no doubt thinking of the desperate nature of the work before us."[30]

At about 10 P.M., Farragut formed up the ships and got under way. The *Hartford* led the line with the *Albatross* lashed to her side, followed by the *Richmond,* the *Genesee,* the *Kineo,* and the *Monongahela.* The old side-wheeler *Mississippi,* steaming by herself, brought up the rear.

As soon as the *Hartford* came abreast of a large pile of wood on the west bank, Rebel lookouts launched signal rockets and lit the bonfire to silhouette the ships for the batteries on the opposite bank. With a loud Rebel yell, the gunners ashore opened fire. The gunners afloat answered. The roar of the ships' cannons accompanied the hissing, screaming, whistling, shrieking, and howling of the Rebel projectiles in a symphony from hell. Smoke soon joined the darkness in obscuring targets for gunners both ashore and afloat. The *Hartford* nearly grounded as she and the *Albatross* rounded the sharp bend. A Rebel shot disabled the *Richmond'*s machinery, and she and her consort drifted back downstream, the *Genesee'*s screw unable to stem the current while lashed to the big frigate. The *Monongahela* ran aground under the Confederate guns. She managed to break free, but overheated a bearing in the process. She and the *Kineo* also drifted back downstream. Rebel gunfire set the *Mississippi* ablaze and killed or wounded sixty-four out of a crew of nearly three hundred.

With the *Hartford* safely past the batteries, Farragut waited for the rest of the flotilla to join him. But as time passed and no other ships arrived, his elation soured into agonizing fear for his men, particularly when he saw the blazing *Mississippi* drifting downstream with her guns going off and shells exploding from the heat. At about 5:00 A.M. the flames reached her magazine and she exploded with a deafening roar. Rebel soldiers ashore cheered. In all, Farragut lost thirty-five men killed and seventy-five wounded. The Confederates lost one man killed and eight wounded. General Banks, meanwhile, had contributed nothing. His men never got closer to the enemy than five miles. On the sixteenth, Farragut penned an apologetic report to the Secretary of the Navy describing the action as a "disaster."[31]

Gideon Welles didn't see it that way. After reading Farragut's after-action report along with those of his skippers, he wrote the admiral to congratulate him on his "gallant passage" of the batteries. "Although the remainder of your fleet were not successful in following their leader," he wrote, "the Department can find no fault with them. All appear to have behaved gallantly, and to have done everything in their power to secure success. Their failure can only be charged to the difficulties in the navigation of the rapid current of the Mississippi and matters over which they had no control."[32] Welles was disappointed by the outcome but not with Farragut, for the man was clearly a fighter. The secretary's congratulations lifted Farragut's spirits. He circulated extracts of the letter throughout the fleet.

At 5:30 in the morning of March 16, the *Hartford* and *Albatross* proceeded upriver. Two hours later the flagship picked up a pair of men from the *Queen of the West* who had been hiding out in the woods since the Rebels had captured their vessel. To Farragut's delight, he learned that the Rebels had lost the *Indianola*. When Porter heard of her capture, he had an old coal barge fitted out with paddle boxes and logs to simulate a gun turret. A pair of smudge pots completed the illusion. That night, Porter cast the dummy monitor adrift. Word soon reached the Rebels working on the *Indianola* that a "river monitor" was bearing down upon them, so they set off the *Indianola*'s magazines to prevent her recapture.

Farragut remained in the Mississippi above Port Hudson for nearly two months. With no Confederate vessels to interfere, the *Hartford, Albatross,* and the Army ram *Switzerland,* which joined them on March 25 after she ran the batteries at Vicksburg, easily regained control of the river between the two Rebel bastions. The ships sent parties ashore to cut telegraph lines and destroy corn, sugar, and flatboats thought to belong to the Confederate government; traded shots with Rebel batteries and snipers; picked up escaped slaves; and intercepted steamers, flatboats, and other river traffic carrying contraband. When the *Hartford* was not under way, Farragut had cypress logs mounted around her about a foot above the waterline, in case an enemy ram appeared, and he honed the crew to a fine edge in drills to repel boarders.

On the day that the *Switzerland* arrived, Farragut sent his son home. Loyall's presence on the flagship had simply become too complicated for both father and son.

During this period Farragut opened communications with Grant. The two met for the first time on March 26 when the general paid a visit to the *Hartford,* probably to discuss the blockade of the Red River and combined operations against Vicksburg and Port Hudson.

Meanwhile, the Navy Department had been receiving reports of an impending attack on the blockaders off Mobile. On April 15, Welles ordered Porter to occupy the Mississippi below Vicksburg so that Farragut could return to the Gulf and deal with the new threat.

These orders dovetailed beautifully with Grant's plans. Porter had already decided to run his squadron past Vicksburg to support Grant, and he did just that on the night of April 16. Grant, meanwhile, cut his men loose from their base above Vicksburg and marched them through the swamps and bayous of eastern Louisiana to a point well below Vicksburg, where Porter's vessels ferried them across the Mississippi to Bruinsburg. From there Grant maneuvered and fought his army brilliantly, ultimately leading the men to Vicksburg's back door, where they dug in for a siege. Porter lingered nearby to support Grant.

Farragut, meanwhile, left for New Orleans on May 8. Four days later he wrote Virginia. "As soon as Mobile and Galveston are away," he said, "I shall apply to be relieved." "I am growing old fast," he explained, "and want rest." [33]

Shortly after Farragut arrived in the Crescent City, Banks finally got his army moving. By May 23, fourteen thousand Union soldiers had dug in around Port Hudson. Farragut's ships provided naval gunfire support through two failed assaults and a two-month siege. Farragut himself divided his time between Port

Hudson and New Orleans, overseeing the river operations, the Gulf blockade, and the logistical arrangements that fueled them both.

During one still, hot day in June, Lieutenant Winfield Scott Schley, who later destroyed an enemy fleet at Santiago during the Spanish-American War, spotted Rebels working on something in Port Hudson's citadel. In temporary command of the *Richmond,* he ordered his rifled gun to open fire. The quartermaster reported a signal from the flagship, but with the signal flags hanging limp and obscured by the smoke from the gun, he couldn't make it out. Schley kept firing until the Rebels dispersed, then went on board the flagship to report.

Farragut returned Schley's salute with a stern expression. "Captain, you begin early in your life to disobey orders," he said. "Did you not see the signal flying for near an hour to withdraw from the action?"

Schley stammered out an explanation.

"I want none of this Nelson business in my squadron about not seeing signals," Farragut said. He then invited the lieutenant into his cabin. Schley was mortified.

Once the door was closed, Farragut softened his tone and manner. "I have censured you, sir, on the quarter-deck for what appeared to be a disregard of my orders," he said to the astonished Schley with a smile. "I desire now to commend you and your officers and men for doing what you believed right under the circumstances. Do it again whenever in your judgment it is necessary to carry out your conception of duty. Will you take a glass of wine, sir?"[34]

In July 1863 the Union achieved two of its greatest triumphs: the victory at Gettysburg on the third and the fall of Vicksburg on the fourth. The latter inspired Abraham Lincoln to pen his famous tribute to the victors: "The Father of Waters again goes unvexed to the sea." The loss of the Mississippi rendered Galveston superfluous, leaving Mobile as the sole remaining port for blockade runners on the Gulf.

The wave of euphoria that swept the North did not immediately hit Farragut. Not only did he feel poorly, but Banks seemed to have relapsed into inaction, despite reports that Port Hudson's garrison had shrunk to only twenty-five hundred effectives reduced to eating their mules.

But Farragut's mood soon lightened. Having run out of mule meat, Port Hudson surrendered on July 9. With his release from purgatory on the river now imminent, Farragut's health improved. Porter arrived in New Orleans on August 1 and, amid much fanfare, Farragut turned over command of the Mississippi to him. Late that afternoon, Farragut departed on board the *Hartford,* bound for a well-deserved rest.

Despite Farragut's frustrations at Vicksburg and Port Hudson and with the *Arkansas,* his overall performance on the Mississippi River had been brilliant. In the face of deteriorating health, the difficulties inherent in operating blue-water vessels in brown water, and his own trepidations about doing so, Farragut made the best of bad situations, followed orders, and retained his aggressive spirit through it all. The Navy Department couldn't help but be pleased with him.

Farragut arrived in New York on August 11. Virginia and Loyall met him at the Metropolitan Hotel for a happy reunion. After leaving his father's flagship, Loyall had received an appointment to the Military Academy and was due to report to West Point on September 1. Virginia had recently returned from a visit to relatives in Norfolk. Farragut had an inexhaustible supply of war stories. There was much to talk about.

After a brief stay in the city, the Farraguts returned home to Hastings-on-Hudson. To thank God for seeing him safely through the war thus far, Farragut contributed the first $500 he received in prize money from the blockade toward the construction of an Episcopal church in town. During the fall he divided his time between home, where he rested; New York, where he oversaw the overhaul of the *Hartford, Richmond,* and *Brooklyn* and rubbed elbows with the commander of the Russian fleet wintering there; and Washington, where he discussed business at the Navy Department.

Gideon Welles found him full of "ardor and sincerity" and possessed of "the unpresuming gentleness of a true hero" and "innate, fearless moral courage."[35] The secretary had occasion to discuss naval leaders with the president a few days later. Abraham Lincoln considered Farragut his best.

While tending to business in New York, Farragut renewed his friendship with Captain Percival Drayton and asked him to become his new fleet captain. Drayton accepted.

On 30 December, Farragut received an urgent telegram from Welles. Reports indicated that Confederate naval forces under Admiral Franklin Buchanan, the first and only officer of that rank in the Confederate States Navy, were planning to launch an attack on the blockaders off Mobile in three weeks. Welles ordered Farragut to depart for the Gulf as soon as possible. "Buchanan has a vessel which he says is superior to the *Merrimac* with which he intends to attack us in a short time," Farragut wrote his son. "So we are to have no child's play."[36] On January 5, 1864, the *Hartford* put to sea in a heavy snowstorm, bound for Pensacola by way of Key West.

Chapter 6

Triumph at Mobile Bay

FARRAGUT ARRIVED in Pensacola on January 17
and found his command in the grip of a strange disease known as
"Ram Fever."[1] At one point one subordinate was convinced that
as many as five Rebel rams were going to emerge from Mobile
Bay, break the blockade, steam up the Mississippi, and recapture
New Orleans.

The main cause of the illness was rumors about the strength
and capabilities of the Confederate ram *Tennessee,* the most formidable ironclad the Confederates had ever built. Laid down at
Selma, Alabama, in October 1862, the completed vessel measured
209 feet in length by 48 feet in beam, drew 13 feet of water, and
carried two 7-inch and four 6.4-inch rifled cannon. She sported
the typical floating mansard-roof appearance of Rebel ironclads.
A nearly 80-foot-long casemate, armored with six inches of iron
plate on the forward end and five inches everywhere else, backed
by two feet of wood sloping at a 33-degree angle, protected her
crew of some 140 men. Her inadequate engines, also typical of
those in Rebel ironclads, could drive her at six knots at best.

By the time Farragut arrived back in the Gulf in January 1864, the *Tennessee* was floating alongside the dock at Mobile, nearly complete. For the Confederates, the last obstacle to commencing operations was floating her over Dog River Bar downstream from Mobile and out into the lower bay.

Farragut had long been gathering intelligence on the *Tennessee* from spies and refugees. As early as February 1863 he had fairly detailed and accurate information on her speed, dimensions, armament, and armor. He had less accurate information on three other Rebel rams said to be ready for service, although none of the three ever were. The only other operational Confederate vessels in the bay at that time were three small gunboats, the *Selma,* the *Gaines,* and the *Morgan.* But Farragut was less concerned about the Confederate naval forces running out of Mobile Bay than he was about running his own squadron in.

Mobile Bay resembled an arrowhead embedded in Alabama's Gulf Coast. Mobile itself lay some twenty miles in from the entrance. The broad but mostly shallow bay measured six miles across near the city and fifteen miles across at the lower, or southern, end. Ships bound for Mobile could navigate through one of two narrow channels past a series of islands lying athwart the bay's entrance. On a spit of land forming the eastern flank of the entrance stood Fort Morgan, a star-shaped brick work mounting 45 guns. Alfred Thayer Mahan considered Fort Morgan "superior in offensive power" to Forts Jackson and St. Philip combined because of its heavier ordnance.[2] On Dauphin Island, three miles across the main ship channel from Fort Morgan, stood Fort Gaines, a smaller star-shaped brick work mounting 26 guns. A line of submerged pilings driven into the seabed extended two miles out from Fort Gaines, and a field of torpedoes moored to the bottom lengthened the barrier to within a quarter mile of Fort Morgan. Buoys marked the dividing line between the minefield and the narrow ship channel. Fort Powell, at the western flank of the entrance to the bay, guarded the narrower and shallower channel through Grant's Pass. The Confederates had 10,000 soldiers to man the forts and garrison the city.

On January 20 Farragut and his staff boarded the gunboat

Octorara and steamed to within three miles of the forts for a reconnaissance. Farragut could see the forts, the guns, and the line of pilings quite clearly. Although he didn't see the torpedoes, he knew from a report forwarded five days earlier that the Confederates had moored across the main channel at least thirty torpedoes, each loaded with seventy-five pounds of powder. He rightly concluded that the obstructions and torpedoes were intended to force ships to steam under the guns of Fort Morgan.

The strength and disposition of these defenses convinced Farragut that both ironclads and troops were needed for the attack. "If I had one ironclad," he wrote in a report to Gideon Welles on January 22, "I could destroy their whole force in the bay and reduce the forts at my leisure by cooperation with our land forces, say, 5,000 men. We must have about 2,500 men in the rear of each fort to make regular approaches by land and to prevent the garrisons receiving supplies and reinforcements."[3]

Farragut envisioned a combined operation in which the Navy would run past Forts Morgan and Gaines and cut their communications by sea, while the Army cut their communications by land. The Navy would then support the Army's siege and assault operations and prevent Rebel vessels from harassing the troops.

Without ironclads, Farragut argued, he wouldn't be able to fight the enemy ironclads "with much prospect of success." It wasn't just their armor that he needed, but also their shallow draft. Without ironclads of his own to root them out, the Rebel ironclads could "lie on the flats where our ships could not go to destroy them. Wooden vessels can do nothing with them unless by getting within 100 or 200 yards, so as to ram them or pour in a broadside."[4]

Ironically, Farragut still looked upon ironclads with disdain. He considered them undependable, unseaworthy, and too frequently inoperable. "Monitors and Rifled Guns are in my opinion demoralizers to men," he wrote Loyall five months later. "They make them think that men should only fight in Iron cases or at 3 or 4 miles distance."[5]

Instead of attacking Mobile in the near future, as he had

hoped to do, Farragut would have to wait. Again. With Banks and Porter floundering about in Louisiana through most of the spring on the ill-fated Red River Expedition to capture Shreveport and gain a foothold in Texas, there would be no troops available for operations against Mobile any time soon. Most of the Navy's ironclads remained bogged down in operations against Charleston under Dahlgren. Farragut queried the Navy Department repeatedly about when he could expect new ironclads for his squadron.

Fox replied late in March. Grant, who had recently become general-in-chief of the Union army, was about to launch his epic campaign in Virginia. If Grant reached the James River, Fox said, the Navy would have to keep a force of ironclads there to keep the army's communications open. "We have the summer before us," Fox said, "and I trust you will not act until you oblige us to give you everything you require."[6] In essence, Fox was warning Farragut not to act rashly before mustering sufficient forces. Meanwhile, Farragut made the rounds, inspecting the blockade and indulging in New Orleans's social life.

Drayton, in fact, thought that Farragut overindulged in the New Orleans social life at times. The city was "still very much of a vanity fair," Drayton wrote a friend on April 8. The admiral "enjoys its life and dissipations as much as any one, never tires of abusing it for the demoralization it produces on the fleet. As for him I can't keep him on board in the evening and he takes me to many places I would be very glad to keep out of." Drayton wasn't referring to bordellos or anything like that; he meant nothing seedier than homes occupied by Army officers.[7]

Although Farragut disdained intemperance, Drayton felt he was partying a little too much for a man of his age. "The Admiral enjoys himself I think vastly here," Drayton noted about a week later, "and would do so much more were it not for the opinion that seems to possess him, that life in New Orleans soon renders a person unfit for the hard life of the profession or at least makes them a little distasteful. We dined yesterday with Mr. Wright, the possessor of the Horse fair, who gave us a first class dinner, which did not hurt me, but coming on the top of a good deal of indiscriminate eating and drinking after the Tableaus of the night previous, rather used the Admiral up." [8]

By early May, however, anxiety over the possibility of the *Tennessee*'s making a sortie against his fleet fixed Farragut's attention on Mobile Bay. "I am in hourly expectation of being attacked," he wrote Gideon Welles on the ninth, not only by the *Tennessee*, but also by the three other ironclads and three wooden gunboats at Buchanan's disposal. A battle between their ironclads and his wooden fleet would be "a most unequal contest," he added, particularly since the *Tennessee* was reported to be shot-proof. "Our only hope is to run her down," he concluded. However the battle turned out, he realized that he stood to lose many men. "I, therefore, deeply regret," he told Welles, "that the Department has not been able to give us one of the many ironclads that are off Charleston and on the Mississippi." [9] Reports that Grant had been beaten and fear that Banks would be captured darkened Farragut's mood. "I get right sick, now and then," he wrote Loyall, "at the bad news." [10]

More bad news followed. The *Tennessee* finally cleared the bar on the night of May 17–18. On the twentieth, Farragut learned that the Rebel ram had gotten down to Fort Morgan. Confederate newspapers reported that Buchanan intended to raise the blockade and retake New Orleans with her. On the twenty-fourth, Farragut and his staff boarded the gunboat *Metacomet* and steamed close inshore for a look at the ironclad menace. She seemed to be everything the reports had made her out to be. Farragut also saw small boats laying torpedoes in the channel. The next day he wrote Welles, repeating his request for ironclads.

Help was on the way. In June, Welles ordered the monitor *Manhattan* at New York and the double-turreted river monitors *Chickasaw* and *Winnebago* at Mound City, Illinois, to join Farragut. In July, Farragut received word that a second single-turreted monitor, the *Tecumseh,* would also be coming. All but the *Tecumseh* arrived by the end of the month. "My monitors are all here now," he wrote Virginia on the thirty-first, "so that I am the one to attack, and no longer expect to be attacked." [11]

The Army sent help as well. Grant had long favored an expedition against Mobile. That same June, he assigned troops from Banks's former command to cooperate with Farragut. The Army had sacked Banks after the Red River debacle. With Grant bogged down in siege operations against Petersburg, there wouldn't be enough troops for a campaign against Mobile. The Army would, however, commit enough troops to invest Forts Morgan and Gaines. The first contingent of soldiers arrived from New Orleans on August 3.

Meanwhile, Farragut readied his fleet. On July 12, he ordered his skippers to "strip your vessels and prepare for the conflict."[12] Farragut had top-hampers taken down, chains or sandbags placed on the deck above machinery as protection against plunging fire, splinter nets rigged on the starboard side, and numerous other details attended to.

Percival Drayton, who had become not only Farragut's flag captain, but also skipper of the *Hartford,* was up to his eyebrows in work. "I never was so worked in my life," he recalled. "Why, fighting is mere child's play compared to the preparations required for it."[13]

Farragut thought long and hard about exactly how to launch the attack. To help him determine the best course, he had his carpenter carve a set of ship models and used them to war-game various scenarios on a table containing a compass rose. Afterward he got the squadron under way several times and had the ships practice keeping close order while changing formation and course.

Farragut was particularly concerned about the obstructions and torpedoes said to be adjacent to the channel. Reports from refugees and deserters suggested that the "infernal machines" had been immersed so long that they had become waterlogged and inoperable. Lieutenant John C. Watson, Farragut's flag lieutenant, made several night reconnaissances to gather intelligence on the torpedoes and other obstructions, but with the considerable area he had to cover and the danger of working close to the forts, he never located any of the 180 torpedoes that the Confederates had arrayed in three parallel lines. It is not surprising that he found no timber obstructions, for they had washed away, a fact that the Confederates managed to keep secret until after the battle. Even though Watson found nothing, Farragut assumed that the obstructions were still there.

Farragut decided to employ tactics similar to those he had used at Port Hudson. Each large ship would have a small gunboat lashed to her disengaged side, so that if enemy fire disabled one, the other could pull her through. He planned to attack in the morning, so that the flood tide would add speed as the ships passed Forts Morgan and Gaines. What's more, the propeller-driven vessels could stop their engines and drift past the obstructions while the sidewheelers kept turning, since the paddlewheels were less likely to get entangled in any drag ropes set for that purpose. The monitors would steam into the bay in a line east of the main column of paired ships. Since they were slower, the monitors would get under way earlier. Once past the forts, the monitors would attack the *Tennessee,* while the gunboats were to be cast loose to prevent the Rebel gunboats from escaping up the bay. While the rest of the fleet passed Fort Morgan, a flotilla of six gunboats would shell the fort from the gulf. Another small flotilla would bombard Fort Powell.

Farragut warned his skippers about the line of buoys in the channel next to the pilings. "There are torpedoes and other obstructions between the buoys," he noted in a general order issued on July 29. "Take care to pass to the eastward of the easternmost buoy, which is clear of all obstructions."[14]

On August 1 Farragut had dinner with Major General Gordon Granger, commander of the Army force assigned to the attack. The two finalized plans for combined operations against the forts. Two days later, Farragut had his skippers report on board the *Hartford,* as he always did on the eve of an attack, to make sure that each one understood the overall plan and his own place in it. Farragut had intended to lead from the head of the column, but the skippers argued that the flagship would be too exposed. They convinced him to allow the *Brooklyn* to lead and to shift the *Hartford* to second place. The attack would commence in the morning.

That night, Farragut postponed the attack for a day because the *Tecumseh* had not yet made her appearance. General Granger's men landed on Dauphin Island to invest Fort Gaines on the fourth, however, as planned. The *Tecumseh* arrived that afternoon. The attack was then set to begin early on the fifth.

In the privacy of his cabin, Farragut penned Virginia a letter of farewell. "If 'God is my leader' as I hope he is," he wrote, "in him I place my trust. If He thinks it is the proper place for me to die, I am ready to submit to His will. . . . God bless and preserve you, my darling." [15]

Well before dawn on August 5, 1864, the ships got up steam and formed columns. 5:30 found Farragut finishing a cup of coffee with Captain Drayton and the fleet surgeon. "Well, Drayton," he said with an air of nonchalance, "we might as well get under way." [16]

The *Brooklyn* led the main column, with the *Octorara* lashed to her port side. Next came the *Hartford,* paired with the *Metacomet,* followed by the *Richmond* and the *Port Royal,* the *Lackawanna* and the *Seminole,* the *Monongahela* and the *Kennebec,* and the *Ossipee* and the *Itasca,* with the *Oneida* and the *Galena* bringing up the rear. To their right steamed the line of monitors, with the tardy *Tecumseh* leading, followed by the *Manhattan,* the *Winnebago,* and the *Chickasaw.* Dawn came at about six-thirty. A southwest breeze was blowing. It would carry the smoke of battle toward Fort Morgan.

The fighting commenced at 6:47, when the *Tecumseh* fired a 15-inch shell at Fort Morgan. Confederate guns thundered in reply. Each ship opened fire upon coming within effective range. The *Brooklyn* opened up at about seven o'clock, the *Hartford* six minutes later.

Despite the favorable wind, enough smoke lingered by the ships to obscure the officers' vision from the poop deck. Farragut climbed up the rigging of the mainmast on the port side for a clearer view. The higher the smoke rose, the higher Farragut climbed, until he found himself almost to the fighting top, some twenty-five feet up. Drayton, who remained on the poop deck, ordered Signal Quartermaster John Knowles aloft to secure the admiral to the rigging. Knowles did so, even though Farragut told him to "never mind." The pilot stood just above Farragut on the maintop, where he communicated through a speaking tube to Drayton below. Lieutenant Commander James E. Jouett, skipper of the *Metacomet*, stood on his ship's starboard wheelhouse so that Farragut could communicate easily with him.

The *Tecumseh* veered from her course parallel to the main column and crossed some 300 yards ahead of the *Brooklyn*. She was no doubt heading toward the *Tennessee* and the gunboats *Selma*, *Morgan*, and *Gaines*, which were lurking above the torpedo field. The other monitors followed the *Tecumseh*. Their low speed caused the wooden column to slow. At 7:25, Captain James Alden, the *Brooklyn*'s skipper, signaled the flagship. "The monitors are right ahead," he said. "We can not go on without passing them. What shall we do?"

"Go ahead," replied Farragut.[17]

The *Tecumseh* had veered so far to the west that, instead of passing eastward of the easternmost buoy, she passed west of it, entering the torpedo field. Five minutes after Farragut ordered Alden forward, the *Tecumseh* rolled over and plunged to the bottom, taking 93 of her crew of 114 with her. She went down in less than thirty seconds. The monitor *Manhattan* passed directly over the *Tecumseh* while huge bubbles of steam broke the surface, survivors flailed about in the water, and doomed men below went through their death throes. The horror of it drove one of the *Manhattan*'s firemen insane.

Farragut watched the catastrophe unfold from his perch in the rigging. He knew that the *Tecumseh* had struck a torpedo. He ordered Jouett to send a boat to pick up the survivors. The *Tecumseh*'s sudden disappearance horrified the Rebels, too. They didn't fire on the rescue boat.

Meanwhile, the *Brooklyn* had stopped. The monitors' veering across her bow had caused the sloop to veer to port as well. She was now heading *for* the torpedo field instead of *around* it. The sudden loss of the *Tecumseh* paralyzed Alden with fear. Oblivious as to what might happen to the vessels behind him, he ordered his ship to back down, lest she, too, strike a torpedo and meet the same horrible fate.

Farragut didn't know that Alden had balked. But he did figure that the *Brooklyn* was having some sort of "difficulty," as he later put it to Gideon Welles. "Tell the monitors to go ahead and then take your place," he signaled Alden, trying to spur him on. Minutes ticked by and still the *Brooklyn* didn't move.[18]

Meanwhile, Confederate gunners, both ashore and afloat, found the range. Their fire grew in rapidity and effectiveness. Farragut saw round after round tear into both the *Brooklyn* and the *Hartford,* mowing men down, splashing the decks with their blood, and scattering fragments of mangled bodies. He could hear the screams of the wounded amid the crashing, banging, and whooshing of enemy projectiles and the thunder of his own guns. He could also see the vessels in the rear begin to press on those in the van. He sensed a disaster in the making.

Something had to be done. Farragut prayed for guidance. God seemed to answer, urging him forward. He decided to take the lead, as he had originally intended. He figured that more torpedoes lay ahead, but meant to steam right through, gambling that corrosion or seepage had rendered most of them inoperable, hoping that the one that had sunk the *Tecumseh* had been the exception. He barked out orders to Drayton and Jouett and signaled the ships behind him to "follow the *Hartford.*"[19] The flagship began steaming past the *Brooklyn*'s port side.

As the *Hartford* went by, Alden reported "a heavy line of torpedoes across the channel."

"Damn the torpedoes!" Farragut shouted. "Full speed ahead!"[20]

The *Hartford* plowed through the torpedo field. The rest of the ships followed. Officers heard primers snapping as their vessels steamed into Mobile Bay. Fortunately, no other torpedoes exploded.

The *Hartford* soon steamed out of range of Fort Morgan, only to confront the *Tennessee.* The Rebel ironclad tried to ram the

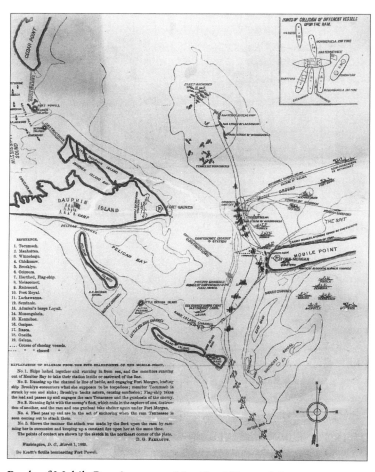

Battle of Mobile Bay, August 5, 1864. *Naval Historical Center* NH63373

Yankee flagship, but the nimbler sloop easily avoided the slow and clumsy ram. The *Hartford* fired a broadside as she passed, but the projectiles simply bounced off the *Tennessee's* side.

The Confederate ironclad also tried to ram the *Richmond,* but missed her, too. She then traded shots with most of the other wooden Union ships as they entered the bay. She remained above the torpedo field after Farragut's fleet steamed by.

Soon after entering the bay, Farragut unleashed the *Metacomet* on the *Selma.* After a hot fight, Jouett accepted the surrender of his Confederate counterpart. Under fire from the Union fleet, the *Morgan* fled and the *Gaines* beached herself in a sinking condition.

The fleet had gotten about four miles into the bay when, at about eight-thirty, Farragut ordered the ships to drop anchor. He had done it again! The operation hadn't gone exactly as planned, however, since the fleet had passed *through* the minefield instead of *around* it. But Farragut's sense of timing and courage to make a tough decision in the heat of combat had saved the day, turning a potential disaster into a great victory.

But Farragut wasn't patting himself on the back. He had climbed down from the rigging to the poop deck, where he and Drayton assessed the situation. "What we have done has been well done, sir," Drayton said, "but it all counts for nothing so long as the *Tennessee* is there under the guns of Fort Morgan."

"I know it," Farragut replied. "As soon as it is dark enough, . . . I intend to go in with the three monitors, myself on board the *Manhattan*."[21] Then they noticed the *Tennessee* moving toward them.

Franklin Buchanan had commanded the ironclad *Virginia* during the battle of Hampton Roads two and a half years earlier. Wounded on the first day, he missed the *Virginia's* slugfest with the *Monitor,* history's first battle between ironclad warships. The *Virginia* fought the *Monitor* to a tactical draw, only to be scuttled after never again challenging the enemy. The Confederate Navy Department court-martialed the man who ordered her destruction, Flag Officer Josiah Tattnall. Buchanan had no intention of allowing the *Tennessee* to meet a similarly ignominious end. Instead of waiting for a better opportunity to arise, he ordered the *Tennessee* to attack the Yankee fleet, figuring that an unexpected dash was the best way to inflict maximum damage on the enemy.

Unlike the *Arkansas,* however, the *Tennessee* didn't catch Farragut with his pants down. The admiral ordered the monitors to attack with their guns and the wooden ships to attack "bows on at full speed." [22] First the *Monongahela,* then the *Lackawanna* rammed the *Tennessee,* doing more damage to themselves than to the ironclad.

Next the *Hartford* tried ramming the ram. As the two ships closed head-on at full steam, Farragut scrambled into the port mizzen rigging above the poop deck for a better view. At the last moment the *Tennessee* put her helm over to avoid a head-on collision. The two ships scraped against each another, the muzzles of their guns nearly touching. Lieutenant Watson stood by Farragut with a drawn revolver, ready to blow away any Rebel sailor that tried to pick off his admiral. The *Hartford* circled around for another try, but the *Lackawanna* accidentally collided with her, ruining the attempt.

Meanwhile, the double-turreted monitor *Chickasaw* worked behind the *Tennessee* and pumped round after round from the 11-inch Dahlgren guns in her forward turret into the ram's stern. With her wheel chains shot away, her smokestack sheared off, her after gunport shutter jammed, a hole blown in her casemate by a 440-pound projectile from one of the *Manhattan's* 15-inch Dahlgren guns, and her skipper's leg broken, the *Tennessee* struck her colors after a fierce hour-long fight.

Quartermaster Knowles saw Farragut return to the quarterdeck just as the dead were being laid out on the port side. "It was the only time I ever saw the old gentleman cry," the sailor recalled. "The tears came in his eyes like a little child." [23]

Farragut had Commander James D. Johnston, skipper of the *Tennessee,* brought on board the *Hartford.* When Johnston reached the deck, Farragut expressed regret at meeting him under such circumstances. Johnston replied that the admiral was not half as sorry to see him as he was to see the admiral. Drayton then congratulated Johnston on nobly defending the Confederate flag. Johnston said thank you, but added that the honor belonged to Buchanan.

Thus ended what Farragut called "the most desperate battle I ever fought since the days of the old *Essex*."[24] Indeed, Mobile Bay was the Civil War's bloodiest naval battle.[25] The West Gulf Blockading Squadron lost 315 killed and wounded, nearly a third of whom perished on the *Tecumseh*. The *Hartford* lost twenty-five killed and twenty-eight wounded. "The officers & crews of all the ships did their duty like men," Farragut wrote proudly in his notebook.[26] The Confederate Navy suffered only thirty-five casualties.

That night, an exhausted but relieved Farragut retired to his cabin. "The Almighty has smiled upon me once more," he wrote Virginia. "I am in Mobile Bay. The *Tennessee* and Buchanan are my prisoners. . . . It was a hard fight. . . . I escaped, thank God! without a scratch."[27] The next day Farragut issued a general order congratulating, praising, and thanking his officers and men.

With Buchanan's command destroyed, the Confederate forts proved untenable. Powell was evacuated on the night of August 5, Gaines surrendered on the eighth, and Morgan on the twenty-second. Thereafter Farragut's squadron settled back into the tedium of blockade duty.

Several weeks later, a caricature of Farragut's being lashed to the rigging during the battle appeared in one of the illustrated weeklies. The drawing amused Farragut, who showed it to Drayton and Watson. "How curiously some trifling incident catches the popular fancy!" he exclaimed.[28]

With Sherman entrenched before Atlanta and no end in sight to Grant's siege of Petersburg, Farragut's victory at Mobile Bay gave Union morale a badly needed boost. Although the city of Mobile remained in Confederate hands until April 1865, the victory ended blockade-running into the port once and for all.

Gideon Welles wanted Farragut to remain in the Gulf to participate in a campaign against Mobile. Farragut thought that taking the city would do no strategic good. Gus Fox wanted him to lead a campaign against Wilmington, North Carolina, the Confederacy's last and greatest blockade-running port. Welles warmed to that idea and ordered Farragut to take command of the North Atlantic Blockading Squadron.

Farragut accepted these orders, but requested leave before assuming the new command. In fact, Farragut didn't like the idea of attacking Wilmington, either, for it meant operating in the shallow Cape Fear River. The nightmare in the Mississippi must have haunted his thoughts.

But the biggest factor militating against his leading the campaign against Wilmington was his health. Throughout the intense strain of leading the West Gulf Blockading Squadron in one attack after another ever since taking New Orleans, Farragut had maintained a tenuous hold on his health. Now, in the wake of his victory at Mobile Bay, he was both physically and emotionally exhausted.

His officers knew it. "I was talking to the Admiral today, when all at once, he fainted away," Lieutenant George H. Perkins, skipper of the *Chickasaw,* noted on August 24. "He is not very well, and is all tired out. It gave me a shock, for it shows how exhausted he is; and his health is not very good anyway." [29] Percival Drayton also knew that the admiral was ill.

Farragut knew it, too. "Few men could have gone through what I have in the last three years," he wrote Virginia a few weeks after the battle, "and no one will ever know except yourself perhaps. What the fight was to my poor brains, neither you nor any one else will ever be able to comprehend. Six months constantly watching day and night for an enemy; to know him to be as brave, as skilful, and as determined as myself, who was pledged to his government and the South to drive me away and raise the blockade and free the Mississippi from our rule. While I was equally pledged to my government that I would capture or destroy the rebel." [30]

Farragut informed the Navy Department about the state of his health at about that same time. "I am willing to do the bidding of the Department to the best of my abilities," he wrote the Secretary of the Navy. "I fear, however, my health is giving way. I have now been down in this Gulf and the Caribbean Sea nearly five years out of six, with the exception of the short time at home last fall, and the last six months have been a severe drag upon me, and I want rest, if it is to be had." [31]

Misunderstandings caused by the slow state of communications between Washington and Mobile Bay kept Farragut in the Gulf for the next several months. In the end, Gideon Welles granted Farragut a leave of absence and gave the Wilmington operation to Porter. Although disappointed by Farragut's need for time off, Welles didn't think any less of him for taking it. "Farragut is earnest, unselfish, devoted to the country and the service," he wrote in his diary. "He sees to every movement, forms his line of battle with care and skill, puts himself at the head, carries out his plan, if there is difficulty leads the way, regards no danger to himself, dashes by forts and overcomes obstructions." [32]

Welles's formal reply to Farragut's request for rest brimmed with grace, dignity, and respect. "A life so precious must not be thrown away by failing to heed the monitions which the greatest powers of physical endurance receive as a warning to rest," he said. "The country will again call upon you perhaps to put the finishing blow to the rebellion." [33] On November 9, Welles ordered Farragut to turn over command of the West Gulf Blockading Squadron "to the next officer in rank to yourself at any time you may see fit and return to New York on the Hartford." [34]

Farragut began the voyage northward on November 30, bringing his active service during the Civil War to an end.

Chapter 7

War Hero

ARRAGUT ARRIVED in New York on December 13, 1864, to a hero's welcome. The *Hartford*'s anchor had barely hit bottom when a group of prominent citizens boarded the flagship to greet him. Crowds cheered as he stepped onto the pier at the Battery. From there a coach took him to the Custom House, where prominent citizens made speeches, read laudatory resolutions, and invited him to become a citizen of New York City. For the next two weeks he and Virginia were swept up in a whirlwind of luncheons, banquets, and other social events, capped by a ceremony in which New York merchants presented Farragut with $50,000 in government bonds.

Farragut's victory at Mobile Bay had catapulted him to a level of fame and popularity never before attained by an American naval officer. Brother officers, American politicians, and world leaders inundated him with letters of congratulation. Newspapers heaped praise on him. Poets wrote verses in his honor. Songwriters composed tunes in celebration of his victories. Even Rebels admired him.

On December 22, 1864, Congress passed a bill creating the

grade of vice admiral. Abraham Lincoln signed it the next day and immediately named Farragut the country's first three-star naval officer.

On the first day of the new year, the Farraguts went home to Hastings-on-Hudson. There they were greeted with a beautiful reception, complete with a triumphal arch erected in Union Square near the railroad station decorated with evergreens and flags and inscribed "Welcome to Admiral Farragut." A large crowd stomped through freshly fallen deep snow to greet the Farraguts as they stepped off the train. Then David and Virginia boarded a sleigh, which took them under arches at street intersections bearing the names "New Orleans" and "Mobile" to the Reformed Dutch Church. As the admiral entered the church, a band struck up the tune of "See, the Conquering Hero Comes." After hearing an address welcoming him home, Farragut rose to deliver a speech. Brimming with emotion and pausing occasionally to collect himself, Farragut thanked the townspeople for their warmth, friendship, and kindness to his family. After the speech he shook hands with everyone in the church, including all the children, then he and Virginia went home.

After only four days in Hastings-on-Hudson, the Farraguts traveled to Washington, where they got caught up in another whirlwind of social engagements, including a dinner with Secretary and Mrs. Welles and a night at the opera with President and Mrs. Lincoln. Farragut also attended Lincoln's second inauguration.

Shortly after the fall of Richmond, Farragut toured the city, stopping in at the Confederate executive mansion, where he found Abraham Lincoln seated in Jefferson Davis's chair.

A few days later, Farragut visited Norfolk. One of the first families he called on had been friends with his own family before the war. When the lady of the house saw who was at her front door, she neither offered her hand nor welcomed Farragut inside, but just stood there staring at him with a sad and bitter expression. At last she broke the awkward silence. "My dear admiral," she said, "between you and me there is a deep gulf." Without replying, Farragut turned away and left. Many of his former friends felt the same way. Farragut cut short his visit to Norfolk and left, never to return again.[1]

It was the same sad story with his Southern relatives. His widowed sister Nancy and the families of his brother William and sister Elizabeth, who had died before the war, lived in New Orleans and Pascagoula, Mississippi. Farragut's role as conqueror of the Crescent City had complicated their lives in unwelcome ways. The admiral had seen little of them during the war, and none had said they were happy to see him when they did, although Nancy had occasionally appealed to him for money. Farragut did what he could, but he couldn't change the fact that the life she had once led as a cotton planter's wife had gone with the wind. Both of William's sons as well as the husbands of both of his daughters had served in the Confederate army. Bitterness lingered after the war, and Farragut lost touch with them all.

News of the assassination of Abraham Lincoln on the evening of April 14 brought Farragut back to Washington. Five days later, six hundred dignitaries crowded into the East Room of the White House for the President's funeral service, including sixty clergymen, the members of the Cabinet, the justices of the Supreme Court, foreign ministers, and Grant, wearing a white sash across his chest. Farragut was there too, "a model of composure and quiet valor," as Carl Sandburg put it.[2] The admiral served as one of the pallbearers.

After these sad events, things slowed down for Farragut, both socially and professionally. For the next several months he rested at home and visited Boston, the White Mountains of New Hampshire, and Washington. He wintered in New York City in a house at 113 East 36th Street bought with the gift from the city's merchants.

The next summer, Congress established the rank of full admiral and President Andrew Johnson named Farragut to the office. The Senate confirmed the nomination immediately, making Farragut the U.S. Navy's first admiral, his commission dated July 25, 1866. Grant became a full general the same day.

Shortly thereafter Farragut and Grant accompanied the president on his "swing around the circle," a tour by railroad of a dozen cities in the Northeast and Midwest launched by Johnson to stump for his party in the fall election. Farragut supported Johnson's conservative reconstruction policy, which provided amnesty and restoration of property (except slaves) to all but the wealthiest former Confederates, returned Southern states to the Union with much of their prewar ideology intact, allowed former Confederates to hold national office, and enabled Southern states to pass oppressive "Black Codes" that so constrained the freedom of freedmen as to return them to a state of quasi slavery.

The tour proved disastrous for Johnson, whose rambling, vulgar, and vindictive speeches mortified his friends and helped the Radical opposition win an astonishing victory that November, including every northern gubernatorial contest, control of every Northern state legislature, and two-thirds majorities in both houses of Congress. The tour proved embarrassing for Grant, who drank heavily throughout and at one point was so drunk he couldn't finish a conversation he had started with Virginia Farragut. The only bright moments in this awkward odyssey came when crowds cheered Farragut at every whistle-stop.

The admiral found his next bit of traveling more to his liking. In the spring of 1867, Farragut received orders to command the European Squadron. Although he was sixty-five years old and not in the best of health, the European Squadron was the Navy's most important peacetime command and a traditional appointment for a senior officer. Farragut had more prestige than anyone in the U.S. Navy, and he wanted the job. On the eve of his departure, Secretary of State William Seward telegraphed him his only instruction, diplomatic or otherwise: "Do not glide too often to the masthead."[3] Accompanied by Virginia, Farragut set sail for Europe on the steam frigate *Franklin* on June 28, 1867.

The *Franklin* arrived in Cherbourg, France, on Bastille Day, July 14. Farragut took charge of the European Squadron during the formal change-of-command ceremony the next day. No nasty political undercurrent or serious problems of any kind marred the next seventeen months. Instead, Farragut had a grand tour of Europe rivaling that of any aristocrat. He dined with Napoleon

III in Paris, walked the gardens at the Summer Palace in St. Petersburg with Grand Duke Constantine, and took in Shakespeare's *King John* from Queen Victoria's box at London's Drury Lane Theater.

At a reception in Lisbon given in Farragut's honor, Portugal's King Don Luis I engaged the admiral in conversation. "You wrote a history of the late war, I believe?" he asked.

Caught off guard, Farragut replied that he had "not turned author yet" and seemed on the verge of getting testy when the American Consul came to his diplomatic rescue. "Admiral Farragut, your majesty," he said, "has *made* the history of the war." [4]

In Minorca, cheering crowds followed Farragut everywhere and treated him like one of their own. This reception thrilled Farragut, for he was proud of his heritage and spoke Spanish like a native. Admiral and Mrs. Farragut also visited Berlin, Moscow, Stockholm, Copenhagen, Edinburgh, Lisbon, Tangier, Madrid, Florence, Venice, Rome, Athens, Constantinople, and dozens of other places in between. They also toured innumerable museums, cathedrals, and historic buildings, enjoying countless dinner parties, banquets, and balls. They rubbed elbows with most of the royalty in Europe and were greeted enthusiastically by everyone else. In various conversations the admiral pooh-poohed newfangled inventions such as seagoing ironclad warships without full sailing rigs and a mechanical contrivance for propelling ships with a kind of piston.

Farragut's tour of Europe ended on October 18, 1868, when the *Franklin* departed Gibraltar for the United States. For all practical purposes, his active service in the U.S. Navy came to an end.

Farragut wintered quietly in New York. Although a Johnson supporter, Farragut, along with Rear Admirals Dahlgren and Goldsborough and Major Generals Sherman, Thomas, Hancock, Terry, and Sickles, attended Grant's inauguration on March 4, 1869.

Farragut's health deteriorated that spring. "The Admiral continues very miserable and I can scarcely leave his side," noted Virginia in May 1869. "I am very much discouraged about him." [5]

Farragut recovered enough that summer to visit Mare Island, California. He wanted to see the navy yard that he had begun so many years before now that it was finished. He spent several days inspecting the yard, looking after real estate investments, and visiting old friends.

Farragut traveled back east on the transcontinental railroad, just completed the previous spring. On the way he suffered a heart attack. It looked bad for a while, but the old admiral pulled through and finished the journey home.

Farragut had several more heart attacks over the following winter. With his health ebbing away, he rarely left home. His doctors thought it might be good for him to leave New York before the hot weather set in. Farragut decided to spend the summer in Portsmouth, New Hampshire. He made the trip, but his health kept deteriorating. He knew the end was near. On Sunday, August 14, 1870, he suffered a paralytic stroke and died at noon.

Three days later, the admiral's coffin was placed in a temporary vault in a cemetery near St. John's Church. On September 30, at a large public funeral attended by President Grant and ten thousand soldiers, Farragut's remains were laid to rest with full military honors in Woodlawn Cemetery in Westchester County near New York City.

Death did not diminish Farragut's fame. Congress named a square for him in the nation's capital and spent nearly $30,000 (in 1880 dollars) to erect there a statue of him, cast at the Washington Navy Yard with bronze from one of the *Hartford*'s propellers. Naval Academy alumni installed a stained-glass window in his memory in the academy chapel. Monuments to him went up in New York, Boston, and other cities and towns. Artists painted innumerable portraits of him as well as scenes of his most famous battles. The Navy named four ships for him as well as streets, buildings, and other features in installations all across America.

"Farragut had a natural genius for war," noted Alfred Thayer Mahan.[6] America's first admiral possessed all the attributes of a great commander: intelligence, confidence, determination, and boldness. He remained aware of the overall tactical situation even as the battle raged around him and his ability to divine the decisive moment for action was almost uncanny.

Courage was Farragut's most prominent attribute. His courage arose from a stalwart sense of duty to God, country, the Navy, and the men under his command. He entered the Civil War with these attributes in full bloom, for they had all blossomed during his boyhood and fifty years before the mast before the war.

Farragut could be gruff and blunt, he didn't hesitate to dress down a subordinate for poor performance, and his enormous self-esteem and love of socializing sometimes irritated superiors and subordinates alike. But he was a good judge of character, confident in his officers' own judgment and abilities, and able to give them the leeway they needed to get things done. Most people, whether peers, subordinates, superiors, or civilians, found him to be honest, kind, approachable, sentimental, dignified without being stiff, and possessed of a good sense of humor. His manners remained simple, yet he had the bearing of someone long habituated to command. The competent officers and men who served under him not only respected and admired him, but also had genuine affection for him.

Farragut's most important victory was New Orleans. The loss of the Confederacy's largest port and biggest city dealt the Southern cause a staggering blow. Although Farragut's victory at Mobile Bay was flashier and bloodier, it had less of an impact on the outcome of the Civil War.

Throughout the war Farragut confronted each problem head-on, assessing it thoroughly and realistically before acting, although sometimes he had to fight the urge to act impulsively. He devised clear and simple plans, and before going into battle, he made sure that each of his officers knew his place in the overall scheme and what to do if things went awry.

Part of Farragut's success in battle rested upon a clear understanding of the era's technology. He denigrated ironclads and rifled ordnance not because he was a Luddite, but because of misgivings that armored vessels and long-range cannons would sap men's courage and offensive spirit. He feared that such technology would encourage engaging the enemy at long distances instead of closing. To avoid face-to-face combat, he believed, was to avoid victory. A pair of his oft-repeated dictums neatly sum up his philosophy on warfare: "The best protection against enemy fire is a well directed fire from our own guns," and "To hurt your enemy is the best way to keep him from hurting you." He was also known to quote French Revolution leader Georges Danton: "L'audace, et encore de l'audace, et toujours de l'audace." [7]

Farragut loved the Navy, but hated war. "War is a terrible business," his son once heard him say. "It is demoralizing and brings out the worst characteristics of men; but we must go to war, or more terrible things may follow." [8] That Farragut excelled at war in spite of hating it remains perhaps the finest example of his courage.

Notes

Abbreviations

B&L   Robert Underwood Johnson and Clarence Clough Buel, eds.
       Battles and Leaders of the Civil War, 4 vols. New York:
       Century, 1887.

LC   Manuscript Division, Library of Congress, Washington, D.C.

ORN   U.S. Department of the Navy. *Official Records of the Union
       and Confederate Navies in the War of the Rebellion,* 31 vols.
       Washington, D.C.: Government Printing Office, 1894–1922.
       All citations are to Series 1.

ZB   ZB files, s.v. "Farragut, David G.," Navy Department Library,
       Washington, D.C.

Note: only the sources of quotations have been provided. No attempt
       has been made to include comprehensive citations.

Preface

1   Loyall Farragut, *The Life of David Glasgow Farragut, First Admiral
    of the United States Navy, Embodying His Journal and Letters* (New
    York: Appleton, 1879), 217.

Chapter 1: Child of the Frontier

1   His parents named him James Glasgow Farragut. He later changed
    his name to David in honor of his guardian, David Porter.

2   Loyall Farragut, *The Life of David Glasgow Farragut,* 11.

3   George Farragut died on June 4, 1817.

Chapter 2: Baptism of Fire

1   Charles Lee Lewis, *David Glasgow Farragut: Admiral in the Mak-
    ing* (Annapolis: Naval Institute, 1941), 47.

2   Lewis, *Admiral in the Making,* 32.

3   David F. Long, "David Porter: Pacific Ocean Gadfly," in *Command Under Sail: Makers of the American Naval Tradition 1775–1850*, ed. James C. Bradford (Annapolis: Naval Institute Press, 1985), 180.

4   David Porter, *Journal of a Cruise Made to the Pacific Ocean by Captain David Porter, in the United States Frigate Essex, in the Years 1812, 1813 and 1814*, 2 vols. (Philadelphia: Bradford and Inskeep, 1815), 2: 62-63.

Chapter 3: Antebellum Naval Officer

1   Loyall Farragut, *The Life of David Glasgow Farragut*, 52.

2   Lewis, *Admiral in the Making*, 142.

3   Lewis, *Admiral in the Making*, 143.

4   Loyall Farragut, *The Life of David Glasgow Farragut*, 133.

5   Lewis, *Admiral in the Making*, 217-220.

6   Loyall Farragut, *The Life of David Glasgow Farragut*, 124.

7   Loyall Farragut, *The Life of David Glasgow Farragut*, 136.

8   Drayton to Dahlgren, August 28, 1853, box 7, John A. Dahlgren Papers, LC.

9   Loyall Farragut, *The Life of David Glasgow Farragut*, 197.

10   Dahlgren to Drayton, October 20, 1859, Percival Drayton Papers, Historical Society of Pennsylvania; Farragut to Ingraham. [ ] November 1859, 1859–61 letterbook, David G. Farragut Papers, LC.

Chapter 4: Triumph at New Orleans

1   Alfred Thayer Mahan, *Admiral Farragut* (New York: D. Appleton, 1892), 55.

2   Farragut's opinions about slavery and African Americans remain a mystery. None of his principal biographers have addressed these subjects. The handful of references to black people in his official correspondence are written in neutral language. It appears that Farragut had none of the virulent racism of officers like David D. Porter, who frequently used the word "nigger" in correspondence, mandated racial segregation aboard ship, and gave black sailors the dirtiest jobs at lower rates of pay than white sailors. The most revealing bit of evidence on Farragut's racial outlook was his relationship with an African American Navy steward, John H. Brooks. Brooks served with Farragut on the *Hartford* from January 1864 onward and considered the admiral a "good friend."

After the war Farragut loaned him $2,500 to build a house in Washington, D.C. Brooks repaid the debt in full, with interest, at the rate of $40 per month. This doesn't necessarily indicate that Farragut was free of prejudice, however, for many slaveowners had warm relationships with house servants. Suffice it to say that the subject of Farragut and race awaits exploration. See Charles Lee Lewis, *David Glasgow Farragut: Our First Admiral* (Annapolis: Naval Institute, 1943), 375, 464, 484.

3   Loyall Farragut, *The Life of David Glasgow Farragut,* 204, 481-82.

4   Lewis, *Our First Admiral,* 9.

5   Lewis, *Our First Admiral,* 13.

6   Robert Means Thompson and Richard Wainwright, eds., *Confidential Correspondence of Gustavus Vasa Fox, Assistant Secretary of the Navy, 1861–1865,* 2 vols. (New York: De Vinne Press, 1920), 1: 299-300.

7   Loyall Farragut, *The Life of David Glasgow Farragut,* 212.

8   *ORN* 18: 48-49.

9   Lewis, *Our First Admiral,* 35.

10   *ORN* 18: 10, 120.

11   *B&L,* 2: 56-58.

12   Loyall Farragut, *The Life of David Glasgow Farragut,* 218.

13   Mahan, *Admiral Farragut,* 252.

14   Loyall Farragut, *The Life of David Glasgow Farragut,* 212.

15   Albert Bigelow Paine, ed., *A Sailor of Fortune: Personal Memoirs of Captain B.S. Osbon* (New York: 1906), 185.

16   *B&L* 2: 60.

17   *ORN* 18: 162, 695.

18   Paine, *A Sailor of Fortune,* 183-84.

19   Paine, *A Sailor of Fortune,* 185-86.

20   Paine, *A Sailor of Fortune,* 190-91.

21   Paine, *A Sailor of Fortune,* 192.

22   Paine, *A Sailor of Fortune,* 193-94.

23   Paine, *A Sailor of Fortune,* 193.

24   *ORN* 18: 157.

25   *B&L* 2: 64.

26   *B&L* 2: 45.

27   Paine, *A Sailor of Fortune,* 197.

28   George Dewey, *Autobiography of George Dewey, Admiral of the Navy* (New York: Scribner's, 1913), 69.

29 Memoir of Ralph Aston, pp. 46-47, file 1, box 1, Ralph Aston Papers, LC.

30 *B&L* 2: 20.

31 Charles S. Foltz, ed., *Surgeon of the Seas: The Adventurous Life of Surgeon General Johnathon M. Foltz in the Days of Wooden Ships* (Indianapolis: 1931), 258-59.

32 West, *Lincoln's Scapegoat General,* 139-40.

33 Mary Boykin Chesnut, *A Diary from Dixie,* ed. Isabella D. Martin and Myrta Lockett Avary (New York: D. Appleton, 1905), 158-59.

34 William N. Still, Jr., "David Glasgow Farragut: The Union's Nelson," in *Captains of the Old Steam Navy: Makers of the American Naval Tradition, 1840–1880,* ed. James C. Bradford (Annapolis: Naval Institute Press, 1986), 171.

Chapter 5: Purgatory on the Mississippi

1 *ORN* 18: 8.

2 *ORN* 18: 705.

3 *ORN* 18: 502.

4 Mahan, *Admiral Farragut,* 178-79.

5 *ORN* 18: 577-80.

6 *ORN* 18: 553.

7 Loyall Farragut, The Life of David Glasgow Farragut, 291.

8 *ORN* 18: 588-89.

9 Loyall Farragut, *The Life of David Glasgow Farragut,* 282-83.

10 Frederic Stanhope Hill, *Twenty Years at Sea, or Leaves From My Old Log Books* (Boston & New York: Houghton Mifflin, 1893), 190.

11 *ORN* 18: 593.

12 *ORN* 18: 595.

13 Farragut, "General Order," 15 July 1862, ZB.

14 *ORN* 19: 8-9.

15 *ORN* 19: 10, 12, 14.

16 Charles H. Davis, Jr., *Life of Charles Henry Davis, Rear Admiral, 1807–1877* (Boston and New York: Houghton Mifflin, 1899), 265.

17 ORN 19: 19.

18 Lewis, *Our First Admiral,* 121.

19 Gideon Welles, *Diary of Gideon Welles,* 3 vols. (Boston and New York: Houghton Mifflin, 1911), 1: 72.

20 *ORN* 18: 564.

21 Still, "Farragut," 174.

22 *ORN* 19: 161-62.

23 Loyall Farragut, *The Life of David Glasgow Farragut,* 394.

24 Loyall Farragut, *The Life of David Glasgow Farragut,* 391; Walter G. Smith, *Life and Letters of Thomas Kilby Smith, Brevet Major General, United States Volunteers, 1820–1887* (New York: G.P. Putnam, 1898), 316. The quotations are a composite of those in the sources.

25 Lewis, *Our First Admiral,* 161.

26 Mahan, *Farragut,* 211.

27 *ORN* 19: 668-69.

28 Lewis, *Our First Admiral,* 172.

29 Loyall Farragut, *The Life of David Glasgow Farragut,* 318.

30 Lewis, *Our First Admiral,* 173.

31 *ORN* 19: 665-69.

32 *ORN* 19: 695-96.

33 Loyall Farragut, *The Life of David Glasgow Farragut,* 366.

34 Winfield Scott Schley, *Forty-Five Years Under the Flag* (New York: Appleton, 1904), 45-46.

35 Welles, *Diary,* 1: 431, 477.

36 Lewis, *Our First Admiral,* 220.

Chapter 6: Triumph at Mobile Bay

1 Thompson and Wainwright, *Confidential Correspondence,* 1: 341.

2 Mahan, *Admiral Farragut,* 259.

3 *ORN* 21: 52-53.

4 *ORN* 21: 52-53.

5 Still, "Farragut," 179.

6 Still, "Farragut," 180.

7 Percival Drayton, *Naval Letters From Captain Percival Drayton, 1861–1865* (New York: New York Public Library, 1906), 48.

8 Drayton, *Naval Letters,* 50.

9 ORN 21: 267-68.

10 Loyall Farragut, *The Life of David Glasgow Farragut,* 399.

11 Still, "Farragut," 181.

12 *ORN* 21: 397-98.

13 Drayton, *Naval Letters,* 67.

14 *ORN* 21: 398.

15 David to Virginia Farragut, August 4, 1864, ZB.

16   Lewis, *Our First Admiral,* 264.

17   *ORN* 21: 508.

18   *ORN* 21: 417, 508.

19   Cornelius Marius Schoonmaker, "Thirty-Four Years in the
      United States Navy," p. 84, box 3, Schoonmaker papers, LC.

20   Lewis, *Our First Admiral,* 269, 469, n. 40. Accounts vary as to
      what Farragut actually said, but the quotation contains the gist
      of his thrust.

21   Lewis, *Our First Admiral,* 274.

22   *ORN* 21: 418.

23   Loyall Farragut, *The Life of David Glasgow Farragut,* 421.

24   "Notebook of David Glasgow Farragut, U.S. Navy, from April 20,
      1862, and Covering the Battle of Mobile Bay, August 5, 1864," ZB.

25   The capture of Fort Fisher on January 15, 1865, cost the Union
      navy nearly four hundred casualties, but most of them fell on
      land during a frontal assault on the fort by a "Naval Brigade."

26   "Notebook of David Glasgow Farragut, U.S. Navy, from April 20,
      1862, and Covering the Battle of Mobile Bay, August 5, 1864," ZB.

27   Loyall Farragut, *The Life of David Glasgow Farragut,* 422-23.

28   *B&L* 4: 407.

29   Carroll Storrs Alden, *George Hamilton Perkins, Commodore, USN:
      His Life and Letters* (Boston: Houghton Mifflin, 1914), 202-203.

30   Lewis, *Our First Admiral,* 291.

31   *ORN* 21: 612.

32   Welles, *Diary,* 2: 133-34.

33   Lewis, *Our First Admiral,* 301.

34   *ORN* 21: 724.

Chapter 7: War Hero

1   Lewis, *Our First Admiral,* 326.

2   Carl Sandburg, *Abraham Lincoln: The War Years,* vol. 4 (New
     York: Harcourt Brace, 1939), 389.

3   Lewis, *Our First Admiral,* 365.

4   Lewis, *Our First Admiral,* 347.

5   Still, "Farragut," 186.

6   Mahan, *Admiral Farragut,* 313.

7   Mahan, *Admiral Farragut,* 289, 315-16, 319.

8   Lewis, *Our First Admiral,* 383.

Bibliographic Note

The purpose of this bibliography is to tell readers who want to know more about Farragut where to look. No attempt has been made to reproduce every work cited in the endnotes or used in writing this book.

The three best biographical works on Farragut are Loyall Farragut's *The Life of David Glasgow Farragut, First Admiral of the United States Navy, Embodying His Journal and Letters* (New York: D. Appleton and Company, 1879); Alfred Thayer Mahan's *Admiral Farragut* (New York: D. Appleton and Company, 1892); and Charles Lee Lewis's two-volume study, *David Glasgow Farragut: Admiral in the Making* (Annapolis: Naval Institute, 1941) and *David Glasgow Farragut: Our First Admiral* (Annapolis: Naval Institute, 1943). The first, written by Farragut's only son, is admittedly biased, but it contains large amounts of primary material available nowhere else. Loyall had exclusive use of many of his father's papers and talked to many of his father's fellow officers. The second, written by the nineteenth century's greatest naval historian, contains the best analysis of Farragut's naval operations during the Civil War. Mahan, himself a junior officer during the Civil War, corresponded with brother officers who had served under Farragut when they were junior officers themselves. The third, written by a Naval Academy professor, includes the most comprehensive and detailed narrative of Farragut's life. Lewis unearthed virtually every scrap of paper relevant to the subject and used many letters that had wound up in private collections. No other Farragut biographer has matched Loyall Farragut's access, Mahan's insight, or Lewis's research.

The finest article-length secondary works on Farragut are William N. Still's biographical sketch in *Captains of the Old Steam Navy: Makers of the American Naval Tradition,* ed. James C. Bradford (Annapolis: Naval Institute Press, 1986) and the accounts of New Orleans by Mark

L. Hayes and Mobile Bay by Jack H. Friend in *Great American Naval Battles,* ed. Jack Sweetman (Annapolis: Naval Institute Press, 1998).

The most comprehensive reference work on "Uncle Sam's Webfeet," as Lincoln put it, is the *Civil War Naval Chronology, 1861–1865* (Washington: Government Printing Office, 1971), published by the Navy Department's Naval History Division, now the Naval Historical Center. Few chronologies reach the level of detail provided in its daily entries, and it's chock-full of illustrations, appendices, and trivia to boot.

Two of the best bibliographic works on all aspects of the Civil War are *Writing the Civil War: The Quest to Understand,* eds. James M. McPherson and William J. Cooper, Jr. (Columbia: University of South Carolina Press, 1998) and David J. Eicher's *The Civil War in Books: An Analytical Bibliography* (Urbana and Chicago: University of Illinois Press, 1997). Either one will take you wherever you want to go in the Civil War.

The most important published primary sources on Farragut appear in the *Official Records of the Union and Confederate Navies in the War of the Rebellion,* eds. Richard Rush et al., 31 vols (Washington: Government Printing Office, 1894–1922) and *Battles and Leaders of the Civil War,* eds. Robert Underwood Johnson and Clarence Clough Buel, 4 vols. (New York: Century, 1887). The *Official Records* include most of Farragut's official wartime correspondence, while *Battles and Leaders* contains accounts of Farragut's principal operations written by participants after the war. Also useful is the correspondence between Farragut and the Assistant Secretary of the Navy in *Confidential Correspondence of Gustavus Vasa Fox,* eds. Robert Means Thompson and Richard Wainwright, 2 vols. (New York: The Naval History Society, 1918–1919).

The principal collections of Farragut manuscripts reside in the Library of Congress in Washington, D.C., and the U.S. Naval Academy Museum in Annapolis, Maryland. Other Farragut papers are scattered across the United States in public repositories and private collections too numerous to list here.

Index

About the Author

Robert J. Schneller, Jr., Ph.D., is an award-winning biographer and historian. He is a member of the Contemporary History Branch of the U.S. Naval Historical Center. Schneller's first book, *A Quest for Glory: A Biography of Rear Admiral John A. Dahlgren,* received the 1996 John Lyman Book Award in Biography from the North American Society for Oceanic History. He also wrote (with Edward J. Marolda) *Shield and Sword: The United States Navy and the Persian Gulf War,* which received the prestigious Theodore and Franklin D. Roosevelt Naval History Prize from the Navy League of the United States, and edited John W. Grattan's Civil War memoir, *Under the Blue Pennant, or Notes of a Naval Officer, 1863–1865.* He lives in Lake Ridge, Virginia.

MILITARY PROFILES
AVAILABLE IN 2002

Farragut: America's First Admiral
Robert J. Schneller, Jr.

Santa Anna: A Curse Upon Mexico
Robert L. Scheina

Drake: For God, Queen, and Plunder
Wade G. Dudley

Eisenhower: Soldier-Statesman of the American Century
Douglas Kinnard

Semmes: Rebel Raider
John M. Taylor